WE SEE EACH OTHER

A BLACK, TRANS
JOURNEY THROUGH
TV AND FILM

TRE'VELL ANDERSON

ANDSCAPE

LOS ANGELES   NEW YORK

First Edition, May 2023
10 9 8 7 6 5 4 3 2 1
FAC-004510-23083
Printed in the United States of America

This book is set in Clarendon URW
Designed by Stephanie Sumulong

Images used courtesy of: pp. 8, 62 Tre'vell Anderson; p. 17
Kimberly White/Getty Images; p.47, p. 213 (bottom) New York
Public Library Digital Collections; pp. 51, 211 (top) Michael Ochs
Archives/Getty Images; p. 77: Ron Galella, Ltd./Getty Images;
p. 100 Vivien Killilea/Getty Images; p. 123 Greg Doherty/Getty
Images; pp. 153, 170 Dia Dipasupil/Getty Images; p. 162 Jennifer
S. Altman/Getty Images; p. 209 Marianne Greenwood; p. 210
Catherine McGann/Getty Images; p. 211 (bottom) Jack Mitchell/
Getty Images; p. 213 (top) Jeff Goode/Getty Images;
p. 214 credit not found.

Library of Congress Cataloging-in-Publication
Control Number: 2022951815
ISBN 9781-368-08173-3
Reinforced binding

www.AndscapeBooks.com

FOR THE TRANSCESTORS
FROM WHOM I, SPECIFICALLY, CAME.
I DON'T KNOW YOUR NAMES,
BUT MY SPIRIT SAYS YOU EXISTED.

CONTENTS

FOREWORD 1

INTRODUCTION 7

TRANSCESTORS IN ACTION: A PRIMER 21

CHAPTER 1:
CROSS-DRESSED
FOR SUCCESS
39

CHAPTER 2:
POSSIBILITY
MODELS
59

CHAPTER 3:
REALITY BITES
87

CHAPTER 4:
LAVERNE
107

CHAPTER 5:
A TANGERINE
GIRL
127

CHAPTER 6:
THE LAVENDER
EXPANSES
143

CHAPTER 7:
LIVE. WORK.
POSE.
157

CHAPTER 8:
MASC FOR
MASC
177

CHAPTER 9:
BEYOND THE
BINARY
195

TRANSCESTORS 209

AFTERWORD 215

ACKNOWLEDGMENTS 221

SELECTED SOURCES 223

FURTHER READING 225

INDEX 226

FOREWORD

ANGELICA ROSS

I DIDN'T WANT TO COME OFF RUDE, BUT I NEEDED TO SPEAK UP. My hairstylist on *Pose* season 1 was just not cutting it. Candy was the character with the kinkiest wig, a texture that many white hairstylists quickly say they can do, but after just a few minutes it's clear they have no clue what they are doing.

I was calm and reserved. I made sure not to come off as an angry Black woman—even though, in that moment, I was all three. I wanted the people behind the show to understand that as a Black trans woman, hair is much bigger than what is written in the script. Our hair and makeup artists help us become our characters. Especially on shows like *Pose*.

We made some headway, and we were understood. We pulled in Timothy Harvey on my hair, a Black cis gay man, and my good friend and established makeup artist Deja Smith, a Black trans woman who has now been nominated for an Emmy twice for period makeup. When it comes to imagery, the person who holds the brush and the palette makes all the difference, literally and figuratively.

The trans community has moments like this every day. In addition to honoring and protecting our own trans spaces, so many of us fight the good fight to make sure others are honoring us as well.

It's a revolution. A daily *human* revolution.

As a Buddhist, I am taught that human revolution means to purposefully engage in behavior that causes a pervasive and radical change within oneself that then has the ability to radically change the world around us. How I move and take action is always with the intention of creating change by being part of the change. The roles I take on in my professional life and my personal life—they must always be done with concern and sensitivity, even when it's not easy. *Especially* when it's not easy.

This means taking a breath. It means being impeccable with one's words and speaking with intention. It means remaining vigilant about the images we create.

This is why we need this book. How transness is portrayed in film and television is a bigger discussion than just entertainment. In transness, nothing is simply a television show or a film or a song or a play. Every word and image and sound is a reflection of our world. And one important question we as Black and brown, queer and trans, disabled communities and beyond ask when we take in any form of media is *Will we be seen?*

The first time I felt seen? Like, the very first time I thought *This is me* in a positive way? It was twenty years ago, and although it showcased true love in a trans space, there definitely was not a happily-ever-after. As far from that as possible.

I was watching a movie called *Soldier's Girl*, released in 2003. It's based on the true story of Barry Winchell and Calpernia Addams. During the height of the "Don't Ask,

Don't Tell" era, a soldier fell in love with a trans woman he met when she was performing at a club. Two of his fellow soldiers mocked him for dating her, and they later beat Barry to death. It was tragic on all levels. And still—

I didn't absorb just the trauma in this story. On-screen, I saw two people in love. Beyond gender, beyond sexuality, Barry and Calpernia were in love in the purest way. It had an impact on me. I was twenty-three years old, and I felt like—*I deserve that. I can have that*. I saw possibilities for myself.

In everything I'd seen before that, even in films or shows I'd enjoyed, the trans character was either a punch line, a joke, a freakish portrayal, or a violent cautionary tale. There wasn't often a balance. There were very few well-written roles with actors who brought trans characters to life with honor and dignity.

I think of the film *To Wong Foo, Thanks for Everything! Julie Newmar*. We would not have three cishet men portraying Noxeema, Vida, and Chi-Chi today. When you know better, you do better.

But! Here's where the nuance comes in. Considering the film's time, I can't take away from what John Leguizamo did in his performance as Chi-Chi. Wesley Snipes and Patrick Swayze were great as well. And even though we all know we'd make different choices today—John Leguizamo said so explicitly back in 2020—there was something about Chi-Chi that many loved.

This is 1995. You have a comedian, a heartthrob, and an action star—all particularly masculine in their films. And no matter what we say about the film today, most believe the three actors came to this film with grace and intention.

Again, today, there are plenty of trans actors to portray trans roles. Whether it always works out that way is another story. As recently as a few years ago, both Halle Berry and Scarlett Johansson accepted transmasc roles. The difference this time? The trans community and our allies were heard. Within days, both actresses not only stepped down from the role, but they also apologized.

That kind of response is relatively new. Slowly but surely, though, people are coming to understand.

When it comes to exploring film and television from a trans perspective, we can't just write a single book and say *Take this and be educated*. It just doesn't work that way.

But books like this one get us closer. They give us a viewing list. They bring all of us, not just the trans community, closer to understanding where we've been, where we are, where we're going.

We all need to understand that transness is a spectrum, and how we are portrayed needs to be handled with class and grace—and most importantly, a willingness to learn.

Speaking of learning, as I write this, I'm just finishing an eleven-week experience on Broadway playing Roxie in *Chicago*. It's a dynamic role in one of the longest-running shows in the history of the Great White Way. It was an honor to be cast, to perform with legends for enthusiastic crowds. There were teachable moments as well.

Do I always want to teach and educate? It can be challenging, but I fully understand my purpose on this planet. It's who I am, and it's what I must do whenever I can.

That's what media does. It slides into us and takes up space, the good, the bad, and the in-between. The images, the words, the sounds shape how we react to the world around us.

We must be so incredibly careful about what we put out into the world and what we absorb.

Get ready for a raucous education. Tre'vell will teach you things while keeping you thoroughly entertained.

Transness is not all doom and gloom.

Every day, my goal is that all the caterpillars are supported in their journey to become butterflies. And as long as I—and Tre'vell—have a voice, our butterflies will have positive, beautiful imagery on the outside *and* inside.

INTRODUCTION

I DON'T REMEMBER EXACTLY WHEN I WAS TAUGHT TO HATE MYSELF.

Maybe it was overhearing family members talk disparagingly about women who "looked like men" and guys who "just want to be a woman," their gender ignorance and latent homophobia and transphobia becoming mine.

Maybe it was in middle school when, for "Crisscross Day," some of the other "boys" and I wore dresses and wigs instead of simply wearing our clothes backward like everyone else. We thought we were so clever, and we were! I also wore a two-inch heel I had borrowed from my mom's closet, a fact she'll first learn about while reading this book. My classmates were shocked and entertained and seemed to have whatever confirmation they were waiting for that I was gay—though I never responded to their prodding.

Or maybe it was earlier, like in elementary school when an uncle punched me in the chest as punishment for standing with a limp wrist one too many times. It stole the wind, and the joy, out of me.

I look back on these moments now, remembering them as violent or ridiculous or both. But these lessons on how to be—or more often than not, how *not* to be—were as casual and everyday as brushing my teeth. It was ordinary to be told in ways large and small that the growing desires of my gender-expressive soul were wrong and an abomination.

I can't say for sure when I learned to be transphobic, or homophobic for that matter, but I know media had a lot to do with it. Sure, my socially conservative family—my granny, who helped raise us when my mom was overseas in the army, was a pastor—had its influence, and the threats of "fire and brimstone" were beyond persuasive enough to keep me on the straight and narrow. But film and television were my escape, my portal through which a world of possibilities of what life could be and look like became real. For many of us, media signals life from worlds beyond. Like energy

Tre'vell's Granny

readings on distant planets, the people and characters we see on screens large and small become glimmers of a humanity and lived experience we perhaps didn't know about prior. A quick survey of the media landscape, however, presents a stark reality when it comes to representations of transgender and gender-expansive communities. And if the cultural productions that have been created thus far are to be our teachers, a record of art and life and existences that came before us, the text at hand is incomplete and flawed. Like unseasoned chicken.

It is the oppressor who, more often than not, writes our collective histories. Or perhaps it's better to say that it's the histories written by oppressors that come to represent a people's prevailing understanding of itself, those written by the oppressed being banned and burned because the real, true tea is just too hot. But the oppressed always find a way, or we make one.

I first thought about writing a book about trans images on-screen in 2015. I was working at the *Los Angeles Times* as a reporter in the entertainment section, which they call Calendar. Though my main responsibilities involved covering movies, by this time I'd already carved out my own, much more expansive beat: diversity in Hollywood with a focus on Black and queer film. Months before the season 2 premiere of *Transparent*, I had this idea to create a fairly comprehensive timeline of trans representation on-screen. I forget the exact thing that got me interested in this project, but it was the same year that Caitlyn Jenner became perhaps the most famous trans person in the world—after Laverne Cox's historic *Time* cover ushered in the "transgender tipping point" and before actress Daniela Vega of *Una mujer fantástica* became the first openly transgender person in history to be a presenter at the Academy Awards ceremony.

I remember searching for a resource like this online and coming up empty. And every time I came up empty, the one person I knew would have some insight was Nick Adams, GLAAD's director of trans representation.

For over two decades, Nick's been silently steering Hollywood in his professional capacity, advising on scripts, supporting casting efforts, and holding folks accountable for their foolishness. When I reached out to him, he provided me with a list of what seemed like every trans person or character who had a meaningful presence on-screen—films and television shows, scripted and otherwise. Some of them I was super familiar with, like Isis King's reality TV stints or that singular episode of *The Jeffersons*, titled "Once a Friend," where one of George's navy buddies has transitioned. Others, like Ed Wood's *Glen or Glenda* from 1953 or *The World According to Garp* from 1982 were news, and new, to me.

With this information, I created the timeline, one where audiences can toggle options to only show them films, documentaries, reality shows, or scripted series. It was and is one of my favorite things that I helped bring to life, largely because I found it to be a rejoinder to sentiments that made it seem like trans people dropped out of the sky when Laverne's historic *Time* cover was released in 2014. That felt like, and still feels like, the prevailing idea, robbing us as a community of our history and providing justification for the ignorant and hateful to further shun, oppress, and disappear us. Because it's a lot easier to look the other way when we're discriminated against and killed if you feel like we're not your neighbor or local nail tech, and are just figments of a Hollywood writers' room.

"Somebody needs to put this in a book," I thought casually at the time. Fast-forward a couple years—during which my gender journey Bankhead Bounced its way further toward my truth and I filmed my interview for Sam Feder's pioneer-ing documentary on trans media representation *Disclosure,* all of which I detail throughout the pages to come—and the thought came back to me as I contemplated a host of ideas for what my first book could be. By this point, trans folks were even more visible in film and television than when I made that initial timeline. And my relationship to those images had changed. Having now grown into my transness, building a more meaningful relationship to and with the images of my community feels important, even vital.

═

I recently sat down to watch *Boys Don't Cry*, Kimberly Peirce's 1999 canonical rendering of the real-life tragedy that was Brandon Teena's 1993 assault and murder, which landed Hilary Swank an Oscar. "How do you write about trans images on- screen and *not* talk about this film?" I reasoned with myself.

But I forgot how violent what happened to Brandon Teena was. I forgot how graphic the film is in depicting that violence. I think I had only ever seen the film in totality once, so this, my second viewing, was startling, to say the least. I was shook—"triggered," as the kids say! I found myself pausing the movie every forty-five seconds as the tension among the characters intensified. By the time I got to the scene where Brandon Teena's body is forcibly exposed to the camera—violently revealing him as trans—I felt my stomach convulsing. I began having flashbacks to the life-threatening and dehumanizing experiences I've had as a trans person.

I watched through the film's end, finally taking a deep breath as the credits rolled. There was one question on my mind: "Now why the hell did you do that?" I sat on my couch unable to move for what felt like ten minutes, trying to process what I had just witnessed and, more important, what it was bringing up for me. I had just forced myself to watch a deeply triggering movie, one that stirs some of my darkest fears around trying to navigate this world in search of the love, desire, and community I deserve. I could've stopped the film at any point when I remembered what I was in for, or when those horrible acts of violence were happening on-screen, but I didn't. Because the goal was to watch, in full, everything I planned to write about in this book—and *Boys Don't Cry* is, again, canonical.

That day, what you are about to read in these pages crystallized; I realized I couldn't write the book I initially envisioned. Doing so would require me to inundate myself with images that are largely traumatic, sensational, and unnerving. Perhaps I might've had the wherewithal to do that if I didn't have to wake up every day and navigate a world that is currently attacking the communities to which I belong. As I write, historic numbers of anti-trans and anti-queer bills are being considered and passed by state legislatures; trans people, mostly Black and Brown trans women and femmes, are still being killed with impunity; and the material realities of my trans siblings, especially those Black and femme, are compromised. I just couldn't volunteer to revisit so many potentially harmful images while it feels like we're in perhaps the fiercest and most consequential-to-date fight for our lives.

And so, in defiance of every attempt to erase my existence and that of my chosen siblings, this book is an archive of my making, of my becoming, and my witnessing. It is a history of trans visibility on-screen, for sure, but hella personal and very much grounded in my realities as a Black, queer, nonbinary bad bitch of trans experience, particularly one who has covered the last ten years of unprecedented trans visibility as a journalist. That is to say that what you read in these pages is through a lens that is wholly mine, and unapologetically so. This book is not comprehensive. It's not necessarily chronological, and you might find that a pivotal moment in our still-unfolding trans cultural canon is not mentioned.

But there are many reasons for that, the most important of which is that those cultural productions likely factored less into my creation of self. And so, while I do hope the words and reflections I share are generative and meaningful to all those who'll read them, this book is not about you—which as I write sounds like the most trans shit ever. . . . "It may not make sense to you, but it makes sense to me, so there it is, then"–type energy. But before you stop reading . . . let me explain.

In June 2020, during what's come to be known as the "summer of racial reckoning" as folks took to the streets in the aftermath of the killings of Breonna Taylor, George Floyd, and Tony McDade, among others, a group of over 150 people—the core of which included West Dakota, Raquel Willis, Ianne Fields Stewart, Eliel Cruz, Fran Tirado, Kalaya'an Mendoza, Mohammed Fayaz, Peyton Dix, and Robyn Ayers—organized the Brooklyn Liberation March. Inspired by a 1917 NAACP protest in which ten thousand people, many dressed in white, stood up against anti-Black violence, the March, which began at the Brooklyn Museum, was expressly in support of Black trans lives. While I was not in New York and therefore unable to attend this historic gathering, I saw the breathtaking images and videos of an estimated fifteen thousand people in all white on social media that day and in those that followed. It was a marvel to witness, even just through my cell-phone screen.

While the gathering featured a number of speeches, it was

that of activist and writer Raquel Willis—who was previously the executive editor of *Out* magazine, where she was my boss—that most stuck with me. You've likely seen the videos yourself, of Raquel, in the Black churchy tradition of call-and-response, leading the crowd through a chant:

I BELIEVE IN MY POWER.
I BELIEVE IN YOUR POWER.
I BELIEVE IN OUR POWER.
I BELIEVE IN BLACK TRANS POWER.

I got goose bumps that very first time listening to Raquel speak and the crowd respond. I get chills to this day, every time I think about that refrain, especially when I need to check my self-doubt and insecurities. That's because I took and take it to heart when Raquel also said, "Let today be the last day that you ever doubt Black trans power."

My Black trans power comes from knowing, in the quiet, undisputed dignity of my humanity, that somebody like me came before, and that because they came and conquered before, so can I. That history, knowing that I belong to a long line of trans bad bitchery, is what keeps me going in the face of all the -isms and -phobias and other foolishness we encounter as a community. Admittedly, it's a history I'm still learning. Because my hodgepodge of public and private school education never taught me that we even existed, let alone names like Pauli Murray, Sir Lady Java, and Willmer "Little Axe" Broadnax. I only learned the names of legendary activists Marsha P. Johnson, Sylvia Rivera, and Miss Major while in community with other queer and trans folks when I was at Morehouse College, not in the classroom. And then when I turned on the TV or went to the movies, the trans and gender-expansive characters were largely unremarkable, one-dimensional renderings meant—perhaps unintentionally, though the road to hell is paved with latent transphobia—to paint gender transgressors as folks *not* to be. Conversations about representation always note that we can't be what we don't see. If that's true, it's doubly or triply so for trans, non-binary, and otherwise gender-nonconforming folks.

So, when I say this book is not *about* you, I simply mean that I've tried to center myself, my Black trans power, to the best of my ability in these pages. Both a means of documenting a history of trans visibility and the impact it's had on Yours Truly, this book is a reclamation of a lineage still in progress, one that can't stop and won't stop. It's a documenting of a transcestry that's long existed in plain sight and in the shadows of history's annals, a hopeful and sober contextualizing of our present moment of increased trans visibility.

I start off with "Transcestors in Action: A Primer." Focused on the existence of folks we'd describe as trans today before, during, and after the advent of moving images, this is for those of you who think Laverne Cox kicked this shit off. Invoking the work of scholar C. Riley Snorton alongside the Black trans histories I first learned of via Monica Roberts's blog *TransGriot*, I also introduce the foundation of my own gender journey, which involved growing up as my pastor grandmother's shadow.

Then, chapter 1, "Cross-Dressed for Success," centers on the tropes trans experiences have been reduced to on-screen, many because of our culture's history with men dressing up as women for comedic and entertainment purposes. Perhaps the most impactful example of this in my life is Tyler Perry as Madea, a character that is both a personal affirmation and a site from which trans-antagonisms arise.

In "Possibility Models," chapter 2, I confront a popular question in our post-#OscarsSoWhite world in service of the ways we as trans folks might sometimes find representation in the very communities and art forms, like drag, with which our identities are often conflated. I honor the likes of Miss J Alexander and André Leon Talley, alongside Patrik-Ian Polk's *Noah's Arc,* as early models of what is possible for the nonbinary trans baddie I am today.

"Reality Bites" is chapter 3 and takes a look at the reality TV space, a place where perhaps the best, most varied images of trans folks happen even amid rampant sensationalism. I revisit Isis King's stint on *America's Next Top Model*, Calpernia Addams's reality dating show *Transamerican Love Story* and Zeke Smith's infamous outing on *Survivor.*

When discussing the last decade of trans visibility, one name likely comes to mind: Laverne Cox. Chapter 4 centers on the Mobile, Alabama, native and the "transgender tipping point" she's said to have ushered in with her *Orange Is the New Black* role. It also charts how she, unknowingly, gave me a new language with which to talk about and see the world.

In "A Tangerine Girl," chapter 5, I detail Hollywood's hypocrisy regarding trans storytelling. Focusing in part on the Netflix film *Girl*, an international film about a trans teen's gender journey that many trans advocates found problematic, I tell a story of how trans film critics and writers helped, in our estimation, tank the picture's Oscar nomination possibilities despite what felt like an organized effort to keep us from screening the film. This was after the industry professed a readiness to do trans storytelling right—or at least better— and be held appropriately accountable following the release of indie darling *Tangerine*, and before trans folks would be gaslit by Netflix's CEO and Dave Chappelle fans.

Chapter 6 is titled "The Lavender Expanses" and recounts my journey to nonbinary bad bitchery. I honor the roles Monica Roberts and participating in Sam Feder's documentary *Disclosure* played in my coming-of-self and reflect on

Monica Roberts

how the visibility of nonbinary folks like ALOK and Asia Kate Dillon aided me.

"Live. Work. Pose." is chapter 7 and zeroes in on the Steven Canals–created, Ryan Murphy–produced series *Pose,* which was another historic moment in trans visibility. But I was skeptical upon its announcement, bracing myself in advance for it to be bad or not truly the momentous happening the headlines wanted us to believe. I'm glad I was wrong.

In chapter 8, "Masc for Masc," I attempt to bring attention to the experiences of trans men and transmasculine people, a segment of our community that is still starving for representation. I discuss the importance of Kortney Ryan Ziegler's *Still Black: A Portrait of Black Transmen* and *The L Word: Generation Q*'s attempt to correct the record.

Uncle Clifford, the matriarch of the Pynk on *P-Valley,* opens the final chapter, "Beyond the Binary," which grapples with images of nonbinary folks on-screen and gender-nonconforming aesthetics in culture. This chapter also features interviews I conducted for a podcast I hosted with *Entertainment Weekly* all about nonbinary visibility, including reflections from musician Shamir, writer and model Devin-Norelle, and authors Jacob Tobia and Jeffrey Marsh, among others.

At the end of each chapter is a viewing guide, curated suggestions from Yours Truly of films and shows that are in conversation with the chapter's theme. Some of them may not be trans narratives per se, instead serving as thought partners of sorts. But when paired with the readings I recommend at the end of the book, these are resources for those of you interested in taking your self-education to new, deeper levels.

━━

Now here is where I'm supposed to explicitly state what I want you to take away from these pages. I'm supposed to say that I hope this book causes you to think deeply about the ways our culture has rendered, quite problematically, trans lives on-screen—and especially how those renderings manifest in the acts of violence and traumas committed against trans folks in real life. I'm supposed to say that I hope my personal stories humanize a trans experience for someone out there who might not know, or care, that they know a trans person, this book being an antidote or cure for their hate. I'm supposed to say I hope this book becomes a useful tool in the fight for liberation and that Promised Land we say we want. . . . And I do hope for all of the above, especially for those of you not Black and trans.

But really, I wrote this book to document my journey of coming into myself alongside the trans and trans-related images on-screen that factored into it, because I wanted to show people like me what our history of visibility looks like when one of us is telling the story. I wanted to show what I have experienced and embodied and witnessed, how I have had to make myself out of the scraps and shreds, the slivers and whispers of representation on-screen. Because I recognize that while visibility can be a tawdry thing, it can also be, and has been time and time again, a radical act in the face of the -isms and -phobias of our society that have led many to believe that we are aberrations, that we are glitches in the matrix of life that must be managed, killed, and erased at all costs.

So, this is the transcestry of *my* making, and in reading what I have documented, I hope that you, the Black trans reader, see yourself and slices of your transcestry. I hope that in centering myself, you feel centered, because, indeed, we see, and are seen by, each other. And for the rest of y'all who read this book not Black or trans or nonbinary, you're welcome.

TRANSCESTORS
IN ACTION

A PRIMER

SOMETIMES YOU DON'T KNOW WHAT YOU DON'T KNOW UNTIL IT SLAPS YOU IN THE FACE. When I think back on my gender journey, this is the best way I can describe the process by which I came into my transness.

I've always had a switch in my walk and sugar in my tank. I'm not sure where it came from, if it came from anywhere. But I remember using my body, at an early age, as a means of accenting my speech and conveying my mood. Yes, in the specifically Black way that all of our speech is accompanied by a side-eye, shoulder shimmy, or otherwise nonverbal expression—but with a little extra razzle-dazzle to make it all my own. Expressing my discontent in words alone was never enough, for example. My entire being needed to let everyone around me know that I was unhappy. Similarly, when I was giddy, my eyes bulged and the smile that my mom will never let me forget she invested so much money in was on full display. This complete embodiment of my emotions came in handy for church.

My granny, Apostle Dorothy M. Holmes, founded her own church in her living room. Initially with only her eight children in tow, she held Sunday service and Bible studies on her own because the church she came to Christ in wouldn't let women into the pulpit. God's Tabernacle of Prayer Church of Deliverance was born in 1998, eventually being renamed God's Tabernacle of Prayer Church of Christian Fellowship. Once the church moved out of my granny's living room, it became one of those neighborhood churches that would have easily blended in with the homes flanking it, if not for the steeple. Granny helped raise me, supporting my single mother, Melliony, when she was away, serving in the army. My granny recognized early that I had personality, and because I was attached to her hip, she's the woman I credit for making me a church queen.

I was my grandmother's shadow. Some of my earliest, and only, memories from childhood are watching her peel dresses and robes out of those clingy plastic dry-cleaner bags, roll her stockings on, and gingerly apply eyeliner and a nude, shimmery lipstick. I would help her choose which hat best complemented her dress, and which turban would truly christen what was always certain to be a rousing sermon.

In retrospect, I learned how to perform in church. I had to perform certain manners, like having to cheerfully greet everyone who entered the building with a hug or handshake. I learned to sing, or more like blend in a chorus because in small churches like mine, the congregation is the praise and worship team; one of the eldest members is the de facto soloist. I also preached, because nobody is too young to spread the good Word.

"Preacher Man" was a nickname I dreaded, mainly because while everyone just knew I'd follow in my granny's footsteps, I knew that wasn't my ministry. Not *like that* at least. But I got the name because of my abilities, or so I remember. You ever seen those videos on social media of a pint-sized child delivering a sermon like T. D. Jakes or Juanita Bynum? That was me, except less dramatic. If you can believe such a thing. I'd preach in youth revivals, speaking to the saints and the ain'ts, just like my granny did each Sunday. I even borrowed a couple lines from her memorable sermons and imitated her speech patterns and inflections to affect the perfect Southern Black minister voice. It was a ki, honey.

I also learned to perform gender in church. While I was lucky that women led the flock and made up the majority of the congregation, the ways in which the traditional Black church stratifies roles and responsibilities based on sex and gender were still present. The ushers were all women. They stood at the door in ankle-length, ill-fitting white dresses, welcoming parishioners, and prepared Communion every first Sunday. The deacons were men who sat on the first two pews and, quite frankly, didn't do much beyond moving the pulpit in and out and helping lead Watch Night Service on New Year's Eve. It was in church that I learned about womanhood and manhood.

There were only ever two genders. And, although within such a binary there was a spectrum of how womanhood and manhood, masculinity and femininity, showed up, it was very clear that those were my only options. And because God didn't make mistakes, the thing hanging between my legs meant boyhood was my ordained present and manhood my future.

Suits were my costume, my way of showing up the way I was told to. And though my queerness came out in subtle ways—a fluorescent, dark violet three-piece suit with matching Stacy Adams gators for Easter, or a pecan brown–and–gold snakeskin blazer with matching pimp hat, slacks and, again, gators for prom—I could easily hide behind just being country.

I held tightly on to that which I was taught at God's Tabernacle until I got to "the nation's headquarters for Black male excellence," Morehouse College in Atlanta. There's a lot I could say about how my time at Morehouse impacted my gender formation, but it all charts back to my freshman and sophomore years. During my freshman year, the college instituted an "appropriate attire policy," a dress code intended to regulate what it meant to look like a "Morehouse Man." In addition to banning sagging and limiting the wearing of hats and durags, it became a national news story because of another tenet that restricted wearing "clothing usually worn by women." It was said by college administration at the time that the latter part of the policy was aimed at "about five students who are living a gay lifestyle that is leading them to dress a way we do not expect in Morehouse Men." A year later, journalist Aliya S. King published in *Vibe* magazine an article about a handful of current and former students who shared their experiences navigating the homophobic and transphobic environment of the school, and broader society, as people whose gender presentations sometimes bucked conventions. Titled "The Mean Girls of Morehouse," it jumpstarted a(nother) conversation about how we treated GBTQ+ students.

"Can a man of Morehouse be gay? Absolutely," the piece's subhead read. "Can a man of Morehouse be a woman? Meet The Plastics."

"The Plastics" was the name given to a group of queer and gender-expansive students whose gender presentations did not follow the masculine expectations of the suit-and-tie image many have when they think of Morehouse; it's a nod to the group of A-listers in the 2004 film *Mean Girls*. These students wore makeup, sauntered down the center of campus in the highest heels, and carried fierce bags and totes. Though the publishing of the article made them the object of ire from countless other students and alumni, they were the first gender transgressors that I could actually touch.

Witnessing the on-campus debate around the validity of their experiences, which felt like folks were calling into question their identities, I distinctly remember feeling like I was on the receiving end of the community's criticisms. Mind you, I was still running from any hint of queerness or transness that I knew was present deep down. But as these conversations took place, I found possibility in the Plastics. A possibility beyond everything I was taught up to that point. A possibility within.

Back then, I didn't know what it meant to be transgender, let alone a nonbinary person of trans experience. But I often wonder how my life might've been different if I had known earlier that other people, like me, were experiencing their gender as something other than what the broader world told them was "correct."

—

When we, as trans people, say that we've always existed, it's often a necessary retort to the widespread and ignorant assumption that trans identity is a newfangled identity. The reality is that trans people, or at the very least people whose gender identities and presentations would be considered "nonnormative" by contemporary standards and definitions, are as old as humanity itself. It's through colonization and imperialism that our legacies were muted, ignored, and in some cases, all but erased. So, before we talk about trans images on-screen and the failures and successes therein, I want you to know with explicit clarity instances of trans existence prior to and during the advent of moving images.

Globally, there is an abundance of evidence that identifies people who, in using today's language, were trans, or at the very least gender transgressive, dating back to at least 300 BC. It's well documented that trans people were in so many ways connected to the Divine. Many were priestesses or other spiritual leaders, and they played an important role in cultures worldwide.

As Leslie Feinberg and Pauline Park note in *Transgender Warriors*, for example, in almost every traditional Asian society, trans people performed a host of religious, or somewhat religious, functions, from the *basaja* of the Indonesian island of Sulawesi (also known as Celebes) to the *paksu mudang* of Korea to other shamans of Japan and Vietnam. And in other communities across Europe, the Middle East, and Africa, not to mention the indigenous cultures of places like Central and South America, gender expansiveness was also not only accepted, but revered. Today, in many cultures around the world, trans and gender non-conforming communities and identities still exist, many of these traditional identities being built into society, offering various levels of legal validation and/or social support for trans or "third gender" folks.

In the United States, one of the earliest documented gender transgressors was Thomas(ine) Hall, an indentured servant in Virginia in the 1620s. Having moved through the world as both a man and a woman, and apparently having had sex with men and women, they faced multiple public and legal inquiries into their gender, including but not limited to community members and their boss sneaking into Hall's living quarters while Hall slept to catch a peek at their genitalia. It is likely that Thomas(ine) was intersex, meaning they were born with a number of sex characteristics that weren't exclusively what we traditionally associate with male or female bodies. But as a form of ridicule and punishment for Hall's purposeful gender transgression, which society deemed a form of deception, they were forced to "goe Clothed in mans apparell, only his head to bee attired in a Coyfe and Croscloth with an Apron before him," meaning they were legally forced to wear clothing associated with men and women at the same time. While many nonbinary baddies like myself might not blink twice at this, never considering it a punishment, this legally binding determination was an anomaly of the period. Though others who were intersex were forced to make a choice and identify as either male or female, the fact that Hall had to present as both in public was purposefully vindictive and meant to be humiliating. Because prior to this decision, Hall was able to change their gender presentation and identification as they wished or needed based on their living and work circumstances, a decision-making process that was as much about identity as it was survival. This court ruling robbed Hall of the ability to make those necessary choices for their livelihood, and it also didn't detail which type of work they could do; this was during a time when labor was divided based on sex and gender, after all.

Hall, who drops out of official record shortly after this legal ruling, is but one example of gender transgression in colonial America, but we know that gender expansivity was prevalent enough for society to start outlawing cross-dressing, in particular, as early as the 1690s—though the laws weren't always applied to folks we might read as transgender today. It's also important to note around this time period, and likely until the late twentieth century in the West, the differences between identities like "lesbian" and "gay" and "transgender" weren't as defined as they are today; queer sexual desires and transgressive gender identities were conflated. In other communities, these identities continue to intermingle in a way that is less neatly parsed.

Countless names come up in the search for folks who contradicted what society demanded of them based on their sex assignment. Look no further than the Revolutionary War (1775–1783), in which numerous women enlisted as men. Perhaps the most famous is Deborah Sampson, who enlisted twice, under the names Timothy Thayer and Robert Shirtliff (sometimes spelled Shurtliff or Shirtleff). Her life story was chronicled in Herman Mann's *The Female Review: or, Memoirs of an American Young Lady*.

About seventy years later, cities across the United States started outlawing cross-dressing, from Columbus, Ohio, in 1848 to Miami, Florida, a hundred years after that. The act of donning clothes incongruent with society's expectations of the sex one was assigned at birth was deemed just as deviant and offensive as flashing others and being nude in public. These laws were a precursor to the infamous "three-article" rule—which required folks to have on at least three articles of clothing that matched their assigned sex—that police used in the 1940s, '50s, and '60s as a means to raid queer establishments and wreak havoc on the lives of LGBTQ+ people.

But the original intention of many of these "masquerade laws" had little to do with gender variance. In fact, it's said that they came into form, in part, to restrict white rural folks from dressing up as Indigenous people as a means of evading tax collectors; the laws were meant to prevent folks from costuming themselves as a means to cover up a crime. Only in the late nineteenth century and twentieth century did they also come to be applied to people we might today describe as trans folks (and drag kings and queens, too). The original intent of the law did not match its implementation.

In 1857, just before Newark, New Jersey, passed its cross-dressing law, literary magazine *The Knickerbocker* published a short story featuring what we'd consider today to be a trans character. Titled "The Man Who Thought Himself a Woman," the piece, which doesn't have an author but is deemed by some as a lost piece of trans literature, offered a rather respectful portrait of an individual who had an unexplainable attraction to "women's" activities and clothing. The work is early evidence of, despite the limited language of the time, a trans imagination in literary spaces.

Then came the Civil War, in which, like the Revolutionary War before it, women and transmasculine folks enlisted when only (cis) men were supposed to do so. There was Albert Cashier, an Irish-born immigrant who fought for the Union. Assigned female at birth, records reflect that Cashier lived as a man long before enlisting in 1862 and well after his service ended. Even though his medical history was violated in 1913 when attendants at a mental institution in which he was committed forced him to wear a dress—the news media got ahold of the story and deadnamed, which means referring to a trans person by their birth name, Cashier in the press—Cashier's former roommates supported him and protested the hospital. When he died in 1915, Cashier was buried in his uniform.

Now, most of the examples of trans identity in America's past that I've mentioned to this point have been white people. That's primarily because the trans historical canon is often told through a white lens, as white people—even the gender transgressors—enjoyed levels of freedom that Black folks didn't. But that's not to say Black folks weren't bucking up against gendered expectations even while enslaved. Scholar-journalist Channing Gerard Joseph has made it part of his life's work to unearth the history of William Dorsey Swann, a man born into slavery who made a name for himself as the world's first self-described drag queen and who should be regarded for one of the earliest displays of queer resistance and liberation in America.

I think it's safe to say there are fewer documented instances of Black gender-expansive folks in American history than our white counterparts. Still, there are plenty enough to paint a picture of what it was like to be Black and trans back back in the day day. Take for example Lucy Hicks Anderson, a Black woman often given the title of being the first trans woman to defend her womanhood in court. Born in 1886 in Waddy, Kentucky, she's most known for being an Oxnard, California, socialite and chef and for running a half block of brothels. Having named herself Lucy by the age of fifteen, her life story became something of national news, even reaching the front page of the DC-based Black newspaper *The Afro-American*, when, in 1945, she was arrested and convicted of impersonating a woman and lying on her marriage license. Her sex assigned at birth was learned after a sailor's claim that he got an STI from one of Hicks Anderson's workers led to an order that everyone, including Hicks Anderson, undergo medical examination. The Ventura County District Attorney arrested her for perjury, to which she reportedly responded in court: "I defy any doctor in the world to prove that I am not a woman. . . . I have lived, dressed, acted just what I am, a woman." As an alternative to prison, she was placed on ten years of probation. But when the government discovered that she had been receiving allotment checks as the wife of an army man, which was deemed illegal because she was trans, the couple was convicted of fraud. After serving her prison sentence, Hicks Anderson and her husband moved to Los Angeles, where she died in 1954 at 68 years old. I claim her as a chosen ancestor because we share the same last name.

There's also Georgia Black, whose trans identity became of national concern only after her June 1951 death, as evidenced by an *Ebony* magazine feature that October with the problematic headline "The Man Who Lived 30 Years as a Woman." While the piece, which was reprinted November 1975 (and reprised in *Jet* in 1989), consistently misgenders her, it offers a look into the life of a woman who was so beloved by her Sanford, Florida, community—the same Sanford,

Florida, that once prohibited Jackie Robinson from playing in its stadium—that Black and white people lined the streets to express their condolences. Moreover, it chronicled how her church family and pastor helped prevent sensational reporting about Black as she died. "Succinctly, Sanford public opinion was divided into two classes: those who didn't believe Black had deceived them and those who didn't care," reads the feature, highlighting just how livable a trans life and loved a trans person could be.

About a year later, Christine Jorgensen, who was white, burst onto the scene with news of her gender confirmation surgery. Though she was by far not the first to use medical interventions—Alan L. Hart, Dora Richter, Lili Elbe, and other trans folks had engaged with the medical establishment prior—Jorgensen is often dubbed the first US trans celebrity, as her return from Copenhagen coincided with media reports of the "Ex-GI [who became] a Blonde Beauty." Some say Jorgensen called the press herself, though she denied it. Her treatment in the news rags of the day, however, is particularly important when we talk about narratives of Black trans folks because of how said Black gender transgressors were treated and considered differently than Jorgensen. Whereas Jorgensen was able to affect a version of white womanhood that made her of interest to mainstream society, Black trans folks whom the press covered in her aftermath were essentialized as "Black Jorgensens" at best.

Two such women are Carlett Angianlee Brown and Ava Betty Brown. They're of no relation, though I like to imagine they would've claimed each other as kin, like Black folks do. Known by some accounts as the first Black American to plan to interact with medical institutions as a means of supporting their gender identity, Carlett was "a 26-year-old shake dancer and professional female impersonator," as written in a June 1953 *Jet* magazine article with the headline "Male Shake Dancer Plans to Change Sex, Wed GI in Europe." But before she was a performer, earning ten to fifteen dollars a night in Boston and Pittsburgh clubs, the Pittsburgh native was a navyperson, having enlisted in 1950 for the sole purpose, she told *Jet*, of getting treatment for chronic rectal and nasal bleeding. The bleeding had been going on for four years, lasting three days at a time and stopping. Upon examination, a doctor discovered that Carlett was intersex "due to the abnormal existence in [her] system of female glands." Though the doctor recommended surgery to remove the glands, Carlett wanted gender confirmation surgery instead, even giving up her US citizenship in the hopes of receiving treatment from Dr. Christian Hamburger, the same Danish endocrinologist who oversaw Christine Jorgensen's hormone replacement therapy in Copenhagen. Christine chose her name as an homage to the doctor.

"I just want to become a woman as quickly as possible," Carlett told *Jet*. She also told the magazine that after the procedure, she intended to marry twenty-four-year-old Sgt. Eugene Martin, whom she'd known since they were kids. He was stationed in Frankfurt, Germany, and the pair had been writing love letters back and forth for almost three years.

Carlett, however, was prevented, it seems, from ultimately having the procedures she desired because the federal government wouldn't let her leave the US until she paid $1200 she owed in taxes. It's unclear if she ever made it to Europe, as her story seems to have never risen to public interest after a final October 1953 *Jet* article that noted she took a sixty-dollar-a-week job as a cook at Iowa State's Phi Kappa frat house. But before that, Carlett was listed as "virtually destitute in Boston," unable to pay a five-dollar bail fine levied after she was arrested for wearing "women's" clothing in public.

In Chicago, Ava Betty was also arrested for wearing "women's" clothing, as she waited for her boyfriend. As detailed in an April 1957 story published in the *Chicago Daily Defender* under the headline "'Double-Sexed' Defendant Makes No Hit With Jury," Ava Betty was found guilty of female impersonation and fined one hundred dollars. The fact that her friends and business acquaintances all knew her as Ava Betty Brown was of no consequence. Though she made clear her intentions, too, to have confirmation surgery in Denmark, she also defiantly said, "Everything I own is in the name of Betty Brown. . . . If I am a man, I don't know it."

The public's handling of the Browns' narratives, to put it plainly, show a stark difference between the lives of some white trans women and those of Black trans women in the '50s. Because of their race, class, and surely many other identity-based factors, they weren't afforded the same ability to be a media darling. And they didn't go on, like Jorgensen did, to be relatively successful actresses, entertainers, lecturers, or authors. They were simply seen as Black Jorgensens, or as the *Chicago Daily Defender* called Ava Betty specifically, "a Chicago version of the Christine Jorgensen story."

Also of note is the lived experience of someone like James (Jim) McHarris, a Black trans man born in Meridian, Mississippi, in 1924. He became of interest to *Ebony* and *Jet* in 1954 after his sex assigned at birth was disclosed during what was supposed to be a traffic stop for improper lights that turned into an instance of diverted police brutality. When McHarris told the arresting cop of his birth sex, in hopes that the cop would lighten up, McHarris was forced to strip in front of a judge and sentenced to thirty days in jail or a fine of one hundred dollars. It's unclear if the charge was traffic- or gender-related. In a five-page *Ebony* feature in November of the same year, headlined "The Woman Who

Lived as a Man for 15 Years," McHarris was photographed in multiple forms of dress, including lighting a cigarette by striking a match on his shoe, with his chest binder exposed beneath an open button-down, and in a borrowed dress and hat, the caption of which carries the McHarris quote to the photographer: "Hurry up, man, so I can get out of this stuff. This is a drag!" McHarris continued living his life as a man, even after the world knew his gender history.

———

I first learned of some of this trans history by stumbling on *TransGriot*, a blog I didn't know at the time was run by Monica Roberts and chronicled the experiences of Black trans folks. I'll discuss how she paved the way for what will eventually become a news media that accurately reports on the lives and deaths of trans people free of misgendering later, but Roberts also used *TransGriot* to tell the stories of our transcestors, revealing to me that Black magazines and newspapers are important archival sites of our queer and trans communities of yesteryear, as is C. Riley Snorton's *Black on Both Sides: A Racial History of Trans Identity*. That's not to say, quite obviously, that the publications Roberts and Snorton reference actually cared about the folks they were covering. Perhaps someone working at these publications did, the transantagonisms present in the pieces simply being a circumstance of the time. But rather, it is to say, yet again, that trans folks have always been here, whether we collectively had the language that we do today or not.

The process of learning this history, the names and stories of, in particular, Black trans folks who've lived before me, has been one of the most empowering things in my life. Even as we enjoy unprecedented levels of visibility of trans folks in popular culture, it's the knowing of a rich legacy of trans life off-screen that has kept me going. Especially in the face of the sociopolitical backlash that is bathroom bills, anti-trans sports bans, attacks on voting rights, abortion restrictions, police brutality, efforts to limit what is taught in our schools about this country's sordid history, and white supremacy's continued vise grip on our society.

This proof of life beyond what has made or will make it to screens large and small drives me and undergirds my desires to question and celebrate, interrogate and uplift, challenge and affirm our understandings of trans visibility. Because this shit is a paradox.

VIEWING GUIDE

KUMU HINA (2014)

About the struggle to maintain Pacific Islander culture and values within the Westernized society of modern-day Hawai'i, the doc shows a very real world where a little boy can grow up to be the woman of his dreams and a young girl can rise to become a leader among men, putting a spotlight on a trans woman who knows her native history.

EQUAL (2020)

A four-part doc series about landmark events and leaders in LGBTQ history that includes a mixture of scripted reenactments and archival footage. Episode 2 of the HBO Max show focuses on trans pioneers, including Lucy Hicks Anderson, played by Alexandra Grey.

FRAMING AGNES (2022)

Agnes, the pioneering, pseudonymized transgender woman who participated in Harold Garfinkel's gender health research at UCLA in the 1950s, has long stood as a figurehead of trans history. In this experimental doc, director Chase Joynt, with stars Zackary Drucker, Angelica Ross, Jen Richards, Max Wolf Valerio, Silas Howard, and Stephen Ira Cohen, bring to life groundbreaking artifacts of trans health care.

GETTING CURIOUS WITH JONATHAN VAN NESS (2022)

An adaptation of the *Queer Eye* cohost's podcast of the same name, this Netflix series has a fabulous discussion of the history of the gender binary in episode 3, titled "Can We Say Bye-Bye to the Binary?" It features an interview with Geo Neptune, the first Two-Spirit elected official in the state of Maine, about how their culture has long embraced gender nonconformity.

CHAPTER
1

CROSS-DRESSED FOR SUCCESS

I, LIKELY, WAS SOMEBODY'S MADEA IN A PAST LIFE. Yes, the brash, Glock-toting matriarch on whose back the Tyler Perry empire is built. There's just something about a woman who allegedly shot Tupac and only prays to God when writing a check that speaks to my core.

My granny introduced me to Madea. I like to think that she had heard from her holy-roller friends about this guy down in Atlanta who had been doing these stage plays that, while rooted in the Bible, had all the drama and energy of a soap opera. On the strength of their recommendation, when the bootleg man who sold DVDs under that highway bypass mentioned he had a filmed copy of the Madea play *I Can Do Bad All by Myself*, she quickly passed him a folded five-dollar bill.

In reality, I don't know if she knew what she was doing by copping this disc. It was the early 2000s and going to the movie theater, let alone a stage play, was a luxury and a usually too-hefty-for-us expense that could be eliminated by waiting a couple days post-release. The bootleg men—because the ones we always bought from were men, it seems—were quick with it, honey. You only hoped that the copy you got didn't have folks walking across the damn picture or too many IRL audience members whose collective laughter ruined the audio quality. No shade, you wanted the copy that was likely filmed at an early showing attended only by folks who got senior discounts.

I Can Do Bad All by Myself is about a gaggle of folks living in Madea's house—Vianne, Madea's granddaughter, who just divorced her abusive stockbroker husband; Bobby, an easy-on-the-eyes chocolate drop who just got out of jail after serving twelve years for drug possession; and Madea's great-grand-daughter, fourteen-year-old Keisha, who resents her mother, Maylee (Vianne's sister). The play is about broken relation-ships, sexual assault, faith, and forgiveness. Throughout the production, different characters break into song: original gospel ditties and renditions of classic hymns. My granny was hooked.

I wasn't immediately enthralled. Though as a baby church queen at the time I loved most of the singing—especially a post–Kirk Franklin and the Family, pre–"Take Me to the King" Tamela Mann—the melodrama was just too damn much for me. The traumatic twists and turns of the narrative, now a staple of most Perry productions, were so campy and hyperbolic that I couldn't truly get into the world that was being built before my eyes. But when I tell you that my whole family got a good laugh out of it!

Sometime later, my mom, Melliony, got her hands on a bootleg of Perry's *Diary of a Mad Black Woman*. Maybe she got it from someone stopping through the barbershop or beauty salon, maybe it was a grocery store parking lot. About an upper-class couple who, from the outside looking in, are living the dream, the play follows the deterioration of Helen and Charles's marriage. When Helen discovers that Charles is cheating on her with her best friend, her mother, Myrtle (Tamela Mann), and Madea come over to cheer her up and give a little advice. Myrtle is the Bible-thumper vehemently against any revenge plot Madea is cooking up. She only endorses prayer and forgiveness as appropriate responses for Helen. Madea, on the other hand, is the type to shoot first and ask questions later. It's at this point in the Madea Cinematic Universe that I fell in love.

My granny, Dorothy, was a local celebrity of sorts, having toured throughout the South as one of the Voices of Thunder, the gospel singing group she had with her siblings. As they all got up in age, the group unofficially disbanded, only coming together, usually, to perform at revivals that my granny staged at her church. God's Tabernacle was officially a nondenominational church, but it gave very much Baptist and Pentecostal every chance it could. My granny also had a radio show on which she'd deliver a weekly sermon over AM airwaves. I'd occasionally join her, reading out Bible verses. Philippians 4:13 was a favorite, and remains one of the few verses I can recite from memory. *I can do all things through Christ who strengthens me.*

Folks just assumed I was going to follow in Granny's path and become a minister. I will say, I do remember my granny hosting a youth revival featuring a slate of young ministers. I seem to recall someone on the program that was easily in her thirties. I wasn't even a teen, I don't think. And if I was, I was barely. I'm not gonna toot my own horn—toot, toot—but I did have a lil' knack for getting the saints up out their seats, all of which I learned from my granny.

Around that same time, I want to say, I began forming questions about the stories in the Bible I'd come to know so well. And as I learned more about my granny's own journey to the pulpit, I realized the ways in which the Bible has been, historically, used to justify the oppression of various communities. The slave masters did it. Men preachers who often lead their flocks to ruin did it. The religious right is currently doing it.

This discovery began my retreat from God and church, in a formal sense, though it was a slow drip. My intro to Madea came around the same time, and to see this character who poked fun at and reinterpreted the Bible for her heathen intentions was extremely entertaining. Hell, it was edifying for a baby queer who knew enough about themselves since age four to know they weren't ending up in nobody's pulpit long-term.

There's a particular scene in *Diary of a Mad Black Woman*, the play, that I won't ever forget. As a retort to Myrtle's hope that her daughter will just pray and let God handle her situation, Perry as Madea riffs off of a Bible verse Mann (as Myrtle) has quoted. "Hold your peace and let the Lord fight your battle." As Madea repeats the Bible verse a few times, she subtly slides her hand into her purse. As she says the verse one last time, she brandishes her gun: "Hold your piece . . ." The audience erupts in laughter. For added measure, after sliding her gun back in her purse, Madea offers a verse of her own. "Blessed are the peacemakers," she says. Then she pulls the gun back out: "Blessed are the piece makers, Smith and Wesson." I had never laughed so hard; hell, it still tickles me to this day.

From there on out, my family and I bought Tyler Perry's plays whenever they came out—even the ones from the late 2010s that trafficked in social-media stars and weren't as funny as their predecessors. And when Madea started getting the big-screen treatment, my family was first in line at the movies, usually on Sunday evenings, I think, starting with 2005's film version of *Diary of a Mad Black Woman*, which starred the legendary Kimberly Elise. Even when the films jumped the shark—cough, *Madea's Witness Protection*, cough—we were there, helping Perry build his empire. And as Madea's -isms, like "Hallelujer!" and "I ain't scared of the po-po. Call the po-po, hoe!" gained popular traction, they were already featured in my lexicon. Up until my granny died in 2016, every time I came home for the holidays, we'd cue up a few Tyler Perry movies and plays, like it was the old times.

Tyler Perry, and particularly his character of Madea, was—and is—embedded in my life. Even as I write this, I own too many of his plays on iTunes, and watch them regularly enough to not be ashamed. But in college, around the release of 2012's not-as-funny and puzzlingly absurd *Madea's Witness Protection* and amid my coursework in sociology and Black feminist theory, I began to make a connection between the types of images we see on-screen and the ways people, in real life, treat each other—and the ways we treat ourselves.

━━

This history of trans visibility is one that forces us to contend with conceptions of identity that don't reflect our contemporary understanding. By that I mean that characters played by men cross-dressing as women, like Madea, are as integral to our discourse as characters played by men, women, or otherly gendered folks that are expressly identified as trans or gender-expansive. So let's start there.

Men have been donning wigs, makeup, and dresses to play woman characters forever. Even prior to the earliest moving images, throughout the late seventeenth century in England and later elsewhere, women were more often than not portrayed by cross-dressed male, usually teenage, actors;

having women onstage was considered immoral. The practice was so ubiquitous there's a theatrical term, "travesti," that refers to an opera, play, or ballet portrayal by a performer of the opposite sex or gender.

These types of roles were present throughout many of Shakespeare's noted works as well as those of his contemporaries. Sometimes there was a comedic element to these characters, which would eventually give way to popular cross-dressed vaudeville acts down the road, or sometimes such characters were romantic leads. As time went on and the grips of patriarchy and sexism somewhat loosened, women would also grace stages, both as women characters and cross-dressed as men.

By the turn of the twentieth century in the United States, female impersonation was a legitimate career path in which men were professionally known for woman characters of their own creation. With its roots dating back to the era of minstrel shows—because where there is racism and sexism, homo/transphobia is right around the corner—the act of cross-dressing in American popular entertainment was not often deemed problematic. During that period, one critic even remarked about Francis Leon, one of the most famous impersonators billed simply as "Leon": "Just as a white man makes the best stage Negro, so a man gives more photographic interpretation of femininity than the average woman is able to give." Which is an absurd statement for multiple reasons.

Speaking of vaudeville, it is from this world of entertainment that many early films featuring men dressed as women got their leads. Vaudeville is a genre of France-born theater performance, but the American version, which author and journalist Trav S.D. notes was "the heart of American show business" for fifty years from 1881 to 1932, was influenced by many "art forms"—and I use that term loosely. Vaudeville performers, S.D. continues, were our first stars, in a modern sense, as people all over the country knew many of their names and they garnered attention from the press, especially for their cross-dressed characters. At one point, there was hardly a week that still-standing Hollywood trade magazine *Variety* did not cover a female-impersonation act.

Of particular note is how most of these characters were purposefully hyperbolic as a means of playing up the comedic factor and distancing the actor from potential allegations of homosexuality. Again, during this time period, words like "transgender" were not among popular parlance; every "nonnormative" identity was all collapsed into "homosexuality." As writer Anthony Slide pens in *The Encyclopedia of Vaudeville*, "there was never anything improper in female impersonation, no hint of homosexuality or transvestism, as there is in much contemporary female impersonation." This was further ensured as the performers took great care not to "swish" onstage, and to appear "suitably manly" offstage. Slide asserts this in light of countless *Variety* reviews that watched for any hint of homosexuality in performances. In an October 1915 edition of the magazine, writer Frederick M. McCloy said, for example, that "the offensive, disgusting effeminate male or 'fairy' impersonator is now in line for expurgation. And the same influences that banish the 'cooch' may be relied upon to kick this odious creature through the stage door into the gutter, where it belongs."

To be clear, it is here to which we can trace contemporary beliefs that trans women and femmes are nothing but men in dresses, and that the practice of cross-dressing should accompany a performance of sorts. That is because someone assigned male at birth and perceived as a man presenting as a woman—to use binary language—was only deemed socially acceptable if it was for an act. To then be perceived as "a man in 'women's clothes,'" in particular, comes with a cultural expectation and anticipation of a show and laughter. The idea that any of these people who got up in drag might be actualizing their true selves was a perverse thought at the time, and the performers made sure that such claims could not be levied their way offstage.

That is how we get to a place in American entertainment where, with few exceptions, men and people perceived as men, especially, dressed up as women might be serves two major functions: The characters they play are either used solely for comedic relief, with the real-life identity of the actor as subtle and overt displays of absurdity; or men don womanhood for the purposes of deception. More often than not, it's a two-piece combo with a biscuit of enacting harm on the side. Film and television reflected and perpetuated these social values as the moving-image industry grew.

Many of the earliest films featured popular vaudeville performers extending their impersonations to the screen, for example. Edwin S. Porter and George S. Fleming's 1901 comedy short, *Old Maid Having Her Picture Taken*, starred Gilbert Sarony, who, according to an obit in *Variety*, was one of the first impersonators of the old-maid type and "one of the funniest men in the show business." The minute-and-twenty-seconds-long silent picture is about a woman who can't get her picture taken because everything in the photo studio is breaking at the sight of her ugly, masculine face. In 1904, Sarony was back on the screen, this time in Siegmund Lubin's *Meet Me at the Fountain*, a six-minute silent comedic short. Centered on a man who is chased throughout town by a gaggle of women responding to his newspaper ad looking for a wife, the film was one of three that year with this same plot. Its main difference, however, was the ending, in which the man falls into a river and is rescued—or trapped, I'd

Gilbert Sarony

say—by one of the women, who, in a final shot in which the pair kiss, is revealed to be played by Sarony. While there is no expressed shock as a result of the reveal, it is clear that it's supposed to be funny. Some have dubbed *Meet Me at the Fountain* as the first trans film, a distinction with which I'm personally still wrestling.

As moving images became longer and more complex, leading up to D. W. Griffith's racist tour de force *The Birth of a Nation*, another early figure on-screen deemed trans appears in his 1914 picture *Judith of Bethulia*. The narrative, about a woman's effort to stop the war, has a gender-expansive character on the periphery who serves as a servant of sorts. The obviously cross-dressed individual is positioned as comedic relief, creating what Oscar-winning documentarian Yance Ford says in Sam Feder's landmark Netflix doc *Disclosure* is another early cinematic instance of the trans joke. But beyond just being laughed at, the character is at the center of what film historians consider to be a historic moment in cinema: that of the first time a cut is used to advance a storyline. During a pivotal scene, the action shifts from the beheading of a man to the trans character waiting outside the tent. As historian Susan Stryker details in *Disclosure*, "the cut trans body presides over the invention of the cinematic cut." The result, then, she contends, is that "trans [imagery] and cinema have grown up together."

By a decade later, cross-dressing was a plot device in and of itself. In 1925's *The Sea Squawk*, a young man poses as a woman to evade detectives searching for a jewel he was forced to swallow by a thief. Then in 1947's *Boy! What a Girl!*, one of what were called "race films" during the time as they featured a Black cast and were made for Black audiences, a female-impersonator character distracts a number of would-be suitors when the woman they were looking for is delayed. Two years later, in 1949, Cary Grant starred in *I Was a Male War Bride* as a French army officer who attempts to pass as a war bride in order to go back to the United States.

Then came the 1959 rom-com *Some Like It Hot*, in which Tony Curtis and Jack Lemmon play musicians who disguise themselves as women to avoid gangsters they witnessed committing a crime. Also starring Marilyn Monroe, the film is cited as contributing to the decline of the Motion Picture Production Code, also known as the Hays Code, which determined what was acceptable and unacceptable in films for public consumption. As you might imagine, anything "homosexual" was unacceptable, so that meant the cross-dressing storyline prevented the film from getting approval. But it was a major box-office success nonetheless and is credited with further weakening the authority of the Code. The film was part of the inaugural class of twenty-five movies that, in 1989, the Library of Congress selected to be preserved in the National Film Registry because they were "culturally, historically or aesthetically significant."

A supposed bright spot in the sea of shitty portrayals we might read as a type of trans representation today was Ed Wood's *Glen or Glenda*—and by bright spot, I mean that it was a film that didn't use cross-dressing or gender non-conformity for purely comedic effect. Though the 1953 picture was commissioned by a producer who wanted to exploit the news and intrigue around Christine Jorgensen's gender affirmation surgery, with Wood as writer and director, the film reportedly became a sympathetic view of trans identity; it was based in part on Wood's own experiences as someone assigned male at birth who wore "women's clothing." Considering efforts he took to emphasize the differences between gender identity and sexual orientation, the film was seen as a plea for tolerance and is an outlier of the period. Some, like famed film critic and historian Leonard Maltin, have called *Glen or Glenda* the worst film ever made, because it was poorly directed and produced. While I wouldn't make this assertion, it is no *B.A.P.S.*

Then came Alfred Hitchcock's *Psycho* in 1960, which is about a shy motel owner who kills the women he's attracted to while dressed as his dead mother. This film sowed seeds of conflation between actual trans people and the transphobic trope of men killers dressing as women. Even though there is a scene in the film in which a psychiatrist clarifies that the main character is not exactly trans, the overriding theme of the picture—which was a huge box office success and nabbed two Oscar nominations, for supporting actress Janet Leigh and Hitchcock as director—that's stayed with audiences is that of a man in a wig murdering people. Considering how few accurate portrayals of gender expansiveness there were at the time, this idea largely went unchallenged, even inspiring to some extent 1980's *Dressed to Kill*.

There are countless other examples I could pull to which we can connect contemporary trans antagonisms, from 1970's *Myra Breckinridge* and 1982's *Tootsie* to 1993's *Mrs. Doubtfire*. But trans women and femmes have never been men in wigs, as our historical pop culture has taught us, purposefully or otherwise, to believe. On-screen portrayals of various forms of gender expansiveness, then, are just as responsible for the criminalization of trans identities as those who enact legislation against us. The entire industry has blood on its hands—but we already knew that!

▬▬

It's a recurring refrain in Hollywood that in order for a Black male comedian to truly make it big, he, seemingly, has got to put on a dress. Flip Wilson did it on his show as Geraldine

Flip Wilson

in the '70s and '80s. Martin Lawrence and Jamie Foxx did it as Sheneneh on *Martin* and Wanda on *In Living Color*, respectively, in the '90s. As did Eddie Murphy as Mama and Granny Klump in the Nutty Professor franchise, the first film of which won an Oscar for Rick Baker and David LeRoy Anderson's makeup in 1997. Shawn and Marlon Wayans in *White Chicks*; Tracy Morgan and Kenan Thompson on *Saturday Night Live*; Miguel Núñez Jr. in *Juwanna Mann*; Brandon T. Jackson alongside Martin in the *Big Momma's House* franchise; *and* Tyler Perry—they all did it in the 2000s and beyond.

Dave Chappelle notably did *not* do it. In a 2006 interview with Oprah, the comedian, who was widely criticized for his overtly transphobic Netflix comedy special fifteen years later, shared a story about refusing to do a scene in a Martin Lawrence movie that would've required him to wear a dress. Despite incessant prodding by the writer, director, and producers, Dave recalled, he stood firm that he was uncomfortable with the idea and ultimately "funnier than a dress." Dave's resistance has since been cited as a rejection of white Hollywood's supposed ongoing effort to emasculate the Black man, cross-dressed characters being a leading example of a mass media conspiracy at work. Now, I might challenge the *intellectual* merits therein . . . but there are plenty of nig-nogs running around who agree, if proven by nothing other than the pilot episode of the Showtime series *White Famous*, which ran for a single season in 2017.

About an up-and-coming comedian, and produced by Jamie Foxx, whose own career inspired its concept, the cable series' first episode centers on an opportunity presented to Jay Pharoah's character to star in a big producer's film as the old woman, à la Madea. Though Pharoah's character finds the idea absurd, he consults a variety of folks, including Foxx (as himself), about the role. During a fantasy sequence in which the character does put on a dress, in a visual representation of said emasculation, his penis disappears.

Dating back to the not-so-long-ago history of this country when Black people were enslaved by white people, it is well documented the ways in which enslavers emasculated, or, some might say, dismantled the manhood of, Black men. Believing them to be physical threats, many enslavers came up with ways to strip Black men of what they perceived was their power. This included everything from castration to death. It's been debated whether or not Black men donning wigs and dresses is castration by another name.

To be clear, in me and mine house, a Black man playing a Black woman character—dress, wig, or otherwise—is *not* an act of emasculation, of an individual or a community. Such a small-minded rendering of identity gives very much hotep energy, and it purposefully ignores and erases the liberatory divinity of the feminine and its ability and necessity to free us *all*. Not to mention, if what we're to understand as Black manhood and masculinity, in particular, can be compromised simply by donning a muumuu or a wig, it is as fragile as it is toxic—and it might not be as worthy of protecting and maintaining as many might believe.

But because so much energy and discourse often begins and ends with a focus on the alleged emasculation of Pookie 'nem, not often enough do we get a chance to talk about the ways in which the women characters these Black men sometimes take on are never afforded the true humanity they'd like to believe is present—even when the characters are supposed to be actual women and not just a disguise. It's not lost on me the ways in which this mirrors how Black women—trans and cis alike—are dehumanized IRL.

For the most part, almost every Black man who is famous

for a woman character they've played has said their characters are inspired by women they, and we, know. For Tyler Perry, it's his mother and aunt. For Martin Lawrence, it was the round-the-way, ghetto fabulous chicks named after luxury cars. The same for Jamie Foxx. While obviously comedy, at the core is *said* to be a love for and homage toward these types of women in our communities. Perhaps this is true. I'm actually sure it is. What is *also* true is that some of these characters are evolutions of what historian Donald Bogle titled his history of Black representation on-screen: "toms, coons, mulattoes, mammies, and bucks."

And this, by the way, also goes for your favorite social-media influencer who's built his following and career off of the same style of characters and caricatures as Tyler and Jamie and Martin and the rest of them. In one way or another, so many of these characters, though not all, ultimately mock a type of femininity and/or patronize a type of womanhood. Maybe not always in totality and just via a joke here or there. But I think it's this confluence of issues—emasculation and how these characters might refract and reflect Black womanhood—that can negatively impact the livelihoods of Black trans women and femmes.

Swirling around every Black trans woman's and femme's coming out and moving through the world is the stench, both recognized and not, of the perceived emasculation of the Black man. To many, our lives are their worst fears made real. They think that we, having been assigned male at birth, were emasculated so much that we want to be women. And then *how* we show up, I think, is sometimes read as a comment on and indictment of cis femininity and cis womanhood—when many of us couldn't be bothered! The result is potential ire from every which way in our community, and when that is put in conversation alongside what I've already detailed about historical conflations between men in wigs for performance purposes and trans people just living our lives, it, then, is difficult to say there is absolutely no anti-trans sentiment in the renderings of many of these characters played by some of your favorite male celebs.

And sure, the transphobia may not be intentional. But when so many of the recurring jokes and narrative beats are about some of these characters' physicality—whether it's their height or big hands or broad shoulders or hairy legs or facial hair, characteristics that, in a binary world, women are not *supposed* to have—I can't help but recognize how the same punch lines on-screen become the very barbs thrown at trans women and femmes to invalidate our lived experiences. And they're used by the (Black) men who are killing us to justify their actions.

When I detail my relationships to various media, I try to make space for the complex and *complicado*. It'd be disingenuous otherwise to not recognize that we, as trans people, can both be entertained by these characters who were foundational in our media diets and question the ways that they are complicit in the ongoing acts of violence we experience.

I'm not sure I'll ever be able to not laugh at the absurdity and comedic brilliance that is Madea, particularly in those early plays. The character and Perry's portrayal are deeply connected to so many aspects of my life that I hold dear—my granny, being a Southern Belle, my love-hate relationship with the Black church, the complexities of Black Hollywood. And yet still, it's important that we all acknowledge how these characters y'all see as just comedic fodder manifest off-screen as sites of trauma, how the ways we laugh at them are connected to how y'all laugh at us trans people for even attempting to live as our authentic selves.

I can say that these characters and the jokes made at their

expense become emotional and physical violence because I've been on the receiving end of them. Hell, I've internalized many of them so much that I throw them at myself before the world gets a chance to. It's what plays on a loop in my mind when I'm trying on "women's clothes" in a fitting room. It's what I think of, quite instinctually unfortunately, right before I leave my home each day, my reminder to arm myself for what may come, said and unsaid.

These tropes we've come to know as commonplace in film and television, and onstage, aren't us, though we're being treated as if they are.

VIEWING GUIDE

MEET ME AT THE FOUNTAIN (1904)

This six-minute-long silent short can be found on YouTube.

GLEN OR GLENDA (1953)

Directed, written by, and starring Ed Wood, this film was once called one of the worst ever made. Some have since suggested it was radical for its time period, as evidenced by its cult status.

"A SHORT HISTORY OF TRANS PEOPLE'S LONG FIGHT FOR EQUALITY" (2019)

This TED Talk by transgender activist Samy Nour Younes asks audiences to "imagine how the conversation would shift if we acknowledge just how long trans people have been demanding equality."

DISCLOSURE (2020)

The Netflix documentary is a moving, in-depth look at Hollywood's depiction of transgender people and the impact of those stories on transgender lives and American culture.

CHAPTER
2

POSSIBILITY MODELS

I HATE THE QUESTION "WHEN WAS THE FIRST TIME YOU SAW YOURSELF ON-SCREEN?" Though it's become ubiquitous, largely over the last five years following the conversation April Reign ignited when she created #OscarsSoWhite, I'm acutely aware that very few people actually want to hear my real answer. While the question is meant to be an opportunity to give flowers where they are due while also appealing to a need for greater diversity on-screen, it seems no one really wants to hear that I've *never* seen myself on-screen. Not the me I am today.

What does it even mean to "see yourself," I sometimes wonder. I've been told it's about being able to turn on the TV and see a face not unlike my own looking back at me. People say it's about ensuring that as many people as possible can find their truths in the characters and people and narratives on screens large and small. They say seeing yourself is about feeling like you belong in society. In my experience, I find that representation has to be about more than just having more Black faces or queer voices or trans aesthetics on display; we need to get to the root, or as somebody's deep-frying big momma might say: *root* (pronounced like soot).

Because in the late '90s and early 2000s, I didn't see myself when I watched Robert Ri'chard as Bobby on *Cousin Skeeter*. I didn't see myself in Saturday morning cartoons like *Recess* and *Rocket Power* and *As Told by Ginger*. I didn't even see myself on classic Black sitcoms of the era, like *Moesha* or *The Parkers*, which I devoured. Quiet as it's kept, I likely was supposed to see myself in a post–*Kenan and Kel* Kel Mitchell's Freddy Fabulous, the effeminate gay fashion student at Santa Monica Community College where Countess Vaughn's Kim Parker is his biggest sartorial nemesis. But though Freddy was clearly gay, he wasn't the star, so what was I supposed to do with a character that only lasted a few episodes?

In the absence of seeing myself fully, I did see piecemeal glimpses of possibility that were transformative. So much so that my typical answer to the question of when I first saw myself on-screen is threefold. First up, I always give kudos to icon Patrik-Ian Polk's legendary television show *Noah's Arc*. Often dubbed a "Black gay *Sex and the City*," the 2005–2006 series of only two seasons and a movie followed the legendary Darryl Stephens as Noah, a screenwriter living in Los Angeles, and his three friends. There was Rodney Chester as Alex, an HIV and AIDS educator; Christian Vincent as Ricky, a promiscuous boutique owner; and Doug Spearman as Chance, an economics professor. The show also featured Jensen Atwood as Wade, a fellow screenwriter who comes out as gay after falling in love with Noah; the legendary Wilson Cruz as Junito, a doctor and love interest for Ricky; and Gregory Kieth and Jonathan Julian as Alex's and Chance's partners, respectively.

"It was the first time that I saw Black queer characters, the majority of them played by Black and Brown queer people in real life, who not only had heartache and pain and trauma, but also had love lives," I told student journalist Chloe Reynolds in 2019 in an interview for the University of California, Santa Cruz's newspaper *City on a Hill Press*. I was reflecting on *Noah's Arc*'s impact on me, among other media, before giving a talk at the college that evening about identity and power in film. "And they laughed a lot. And they went to brunch. They were able to have jobs. Yes, they got beat up and they got gay-bashed, but they also were able to just walk down the street and buy cars and live life and do those mundane things that up to that point, I had never seen Black, queer people being able to do. . . . I wanted to be a lawyer because Elle Woods [played by Reese Witherspoon in *Legally Blonde*] was a lawyer. And I wanted to be happy because I saw it on *Noah's Arc*."

While definitely ahead of its time, *Noah's Arc* still stands as one of few, if not the only, scripted series to be centered on Black gay men. And though shows like *Empire* and *Pose* have definitely pushed the envelope of what Black LGBTQ+ storytelling can look like, Polk's series—which he also wrote and directed—is by far the prototype and has, in my opinion, yet to be topped. The web series *For the Boys* comes closest. Co-created by Mekhai Lee and Ellis C. Dawson, it follows the lives of three young, queer Black friends—Drew Coleman as Jamal, Chandler Bryant as Anthony, and Lamont Walker II as Syed—as they navigate love and friendship in New York City.

In addition to *Noah's Arc*, I also give flowers to Miss J Alexander and André Leon Talley, both of whom came into my consciousness via the Tyra Banks–created and -hosted *America's Next Top Model*. I still remember Miss J's first episode, in which the long-legged beauty arrived on set in just a T-shirt and heels. And when famed *Vogue* editor and fashion journalist André Leon Talley joined the show thirteen years later, he, too, shook something in me.

As I wrote in the *Los Angeles Times* upon learning the series was ending in 2015 after twenty-two cycles: "Miss J. was the 'runway diva extraordinaire' who shepherded the catwalks of supermodels Naomi Campbell and Kimora Lee Simmons, among others. His skill was unmatched in turning gangly ducklings into graceful swans with the very click-clack of his stilettos." Talley was legendary in his own right for breaking glass ceilings during his thirty-year stint at *Vogue* magazine. His voice, a deep yet feminine tremble, and six-foot-six frame on the *Top Model* set well accented his perfectly coiffed salt-and-pepper fade. He commanded attention.

And though Mr. J, aka Jay Manuel, was in the mix, too—his now-trademark and perfectly sculpted silver hair shining brighter than a pile of new nickels since cycle 2—it was Miss

Tre'vell and André Leon Talley

J and André whose presentations most resonated with my inner gender bender clamoring for liberation. I didn't just want to be like them; I wanted to *be* them. I wanted to walk into a room and stun folks with my confidence. I wanted to trample popular conceptions of Black masculinity with every step I took in a pair of heels. But I couldn't act on it. Seeing them do so, however, gave me hope of a future to come.

At the intersection of *Noah's Arc* and *ANTM* is where I locate a younger me who felt seen and held by what they saw on television. In many ways, because of them, I had accepted that I was queer—or gay, and later gender non-conforming, as I didn't have other language at the time—long before asserting myself as a nonbinary bad bitch of trans experience. The collection of those images did something for me, "for this lil' sissy boy from South Carolina with an imagination far beyond the confines of my Black and conservative lineage," as I continued in the *LA Times*.

But upon deeper reflection and introspection, I didn't *really* see myself in them, not the me I am today. I don't say that to delegitimize or minimize their impact, on me or anyone else for that matter. Rather, I just want to properly categorize it. I think my connections to Noah and his friends, and Miss J and ALT, are less about what they showed me on-screen and more about the imagination within me they unlocked.

These Black gay men who were played, written, and directed by a Black gay man, alongside a Black gay diva and famed editor who didn't, in fact, explicitly identify as LGBTQ+ but was welcomed by the community nonetheless were access points. They were models of possibilities.

====

The lens through which we most often view trans representation sometimes fails us. In an effort to toe a line in which we don't embolden transphobic definitions of our humanity, we sometimes leave out sites of visibility that might complicate a person's understanding of us, and our understanding of ourselves. I think this is why we don't often consider, and why some might see it as against type, to be writing about (presumed cis male) drag queens in a book about trans representation. I get it, especially because trans people are not drag queens, even as some drag queens and other drag artists are trans. But historically, people that we might consider or describe as trans or gender-expansive today were called, among other things, drag queens. Many, like activist Marsha P. Johnson, for example, called themselves drag queens. Sometimes the term described the now-mainstream art of performance as seen on shows like *RuPaul's Drag Race*. Other times, people embraced the ill-fitted language for their personal identities, rebuffing traditional conceptions of manhood and womanhood and evidence of identities beyond. Perhaps they were early embodiments of the famous RuPaul saying "We're all born naked and the rest is drag."

That said, I think it's important to review images of characters we believe are drag queens as models of possibility in pursuit of unknown or unacknowledged trans visibility. Is a character really a drag queen if we never see them out of drag? Perhaps. Is there a chance that characters described as drag queens on-screen are actually stand-ins for trans women? I think so. Did Hollywood call these characters "drag queens" because other terms were less marketable? Almost certainly, and that would be an instance of the ways our stories and experiences as trans folks are often sanitized, repackaged, and made palatable for mass consumption.

Take, for example, the Clint Eastwood–directed *Midnight in the Garden of Good and Evil*. The 1997 mystery drama, based on John Berendt's 1994 "nonfiction novel" of the same name, follows an antiques dealer (Kevin Spacey) who is on trial for the murder of a male lover who happens to be a sex worker. John Cusack plays a journalist interested in writing a book about the case and the cast of characters he meets in the coastal Georgia town of Savannah. One of those characters is Chablis Deveau, based on the real-life The Lady Chablis, to whom a whole chapter in Berendt's book is dedicated and who successfully campaigned to play the version of herself in the film.

On-screen, Chablis is only ever described as a drag queen. Host of a show at a local gay bar, she comes into the life of Cusack's journalist during his search for people who knew the murdered man. When Cusack arrives at a house where he believes the man lived, which is listed in the phone book as the home of "F. Deveau," he meets Chablis. She turns him away, and later they cross paths on the street as Chablis is leaving one of her weekly appointments for estrogen shots. After weaseling her way into a ride home from Cusack, he asks her about the phone-book listing. She reveals that the "F." is for Frank, which is only momentarily perplexing to Cusack's character—after all, he's a writer from up north. The rest of the Savannah community, however, has a palpable disdain for Chablis and her kind of folks.

As the court case at the center of the film unfolds, we learn more about Chablis—elements that, in addition to the estrogen shots, forecast the character's transness even though said language is never used. More often than not, she's referred to using feminine pronouns. If she's not, those people are not only corrected, but they acknowledge Chablis's understanding of herself—even if they're visibly upset or uncomfortable. There's even a number of conversations between Chablis and Cusack's character about Chablis "hiding [her] candy" and him not "telling [her] tea." When she's called to be a witness in the court case, Cusack warns her that the intention is to embarrass her in pursuit of a conviction. She quips: "Them folks think they're using The Doll, but The Doll is using them right back. I'm gonna use that courtroom as my coming-out party." And that she did!

We consider *Midnight in the Garden of Good and Evil* a largely positive image of trans representation on film, and that makes sense; Chablis played a version of herself, a character who is allowed to, though not without pushback, assert her truth and evades the life-ending trauma and violence that often comes to Black trans folks in popular culture. But the transness of the character is largely subtext, a collection of whispers and comedic innuendos that we've ascribed a trans identity to because of the in-real-life ways The Lady Chablis carried herself. Articles of the time period, for example—the book made her a local and cult celebrity, a status that only ballooned after the film released and around the same time of which she released her book *Hiding My Candy: The Autobiography of the Grand Empress of Savannah*—describe The Lady Chablis as everything from "a full-time transvestite" to "a preoperative transsexual." The text of the film, on the other hand, renders the on-screen portrayal only ever, in title, as a drag queen. I should note here that The Lady Chablis did not like the term "drag queen." She told a journalist back in 1998: "I usually refer to myself as a female impersonator. People who call me a drag queen just don't know what they're talking about."

Two years prior to *Midnight*, another film spotlighted drag characters. The Beeban Kidron–directed road-trip comedy *To Wong Foo, Thanks for Everything! Julie Newmar* starred Wesley Snipes as Noxeema Jackson, Patrick Swayze as Vida Boheme, and John Leguizamo as Chi-Chi Rodriguez, three New York City drag queens who drive cross-country to Los

Angeles for a large competition. Written by Douglas Carter Beane, the 1995 picture was inspired by the 1992 anti-gay propaganda movie *The Gay Agenda*.

"There was a line in it where they had these drag queens at a pride parade, asking, 'Do you want these drag queens in *your* town, America?'" Beane told *Today* in 2020, the film's twenty-fifth anniversary. "And I thought to myself, 'Yes! You need these queens. Someone needs to get in there and just shake you up, baby, and show you a little color, dance, life, and a little love.'"

Initially intended to be a stage play, that idea was halted when Beane couldn't figure out how to get a car onstage. *To Wong Foo* became his first screenplay, and upon its completion, Mitch Kohn, an openly gay film executive, put the script in front of his boss at Amblin Entertainment, Steven Spielberg. Yes, *that* Steven Spielberg. As the lore goes, Spielberg read the script that night and loved it. Unfazed by "the gay stuff," as Kohn wrote in the *Advocate* in 2015, Spielberg sent the script to a comedy friend to see if the story was as funny as he thought. That friend, the famed Robin Williams, who was fresh off the second-highest-grossing film worldwide of 1993, *Mrs. Doubtfire*—a movie in which he plays a recently divorced father who cross-dresses as an old lady housekeeper to be able to interact with his children—told Spielberg to make the movie. According to Kohn, Williams said he couldn't star in the film because he was too hairy, but agreed to make a cameo. Said cameo is uncredited because Williams didn't want to take attention away from the film's stars.

In case you haven't seen *To Wong Foo*—which, come on now!—the main plot is that as the queens are driving across the country, they get pulled over by a cop that apparently can't tell they aren't women. That is, until he sexually assaults

Vida and she unintentionally knocks the cop unconscious. The queens flee into the fictional small town of Snydersville, Nebraska, where they must wait it out until a part for their busted car is retrieved by the local mechanic. By the time the cop finds them, the ladies have won over the townspeople who were initially skeptical of them and the townsfolk actually run the cop out of their town.

The entire conceit of the film is that some people see the trio as gay men in drag, an art form that was taboo, frowned upon, and cause for violence. Meanwhile, many others see Vida, Noxeema, and Chi-Chi as women. For example, when the trio make their first pit stop at a motel and Chi-Chi rushes into the establishment, determined to get a room despite the older queens' trepidation about how they might be received, they're greeted by the manager. Thinking they'd be turned away, the manager instead escorts them to a room where their "friends" are. In the next scene, they're among a group of women where a posted sign reads LADIES' BASKETBALL LEAGUE. And in the scene after that, Noxeema is playing basketball with the women, a likely callback to Snipes's role as a basketball player in *White Men Can't Jump* three years earlier. Now, this surely-intended-as-cheeky moment is either sexist or transphobic or both, but it also illustrates a supposed "passability" of the characters as indeed women, albeit more masculine ones, as the scene implies, and not men in drag. Mind you, we also never see the queens de-drag or out of drag, save the first couple minutes of the movie, when Vida steps out of the shower into a montage of her and Noxeema getting dolled up.

There is mainly one scene that explicitly references transness in *To Wong Foo*, which could easily be the single source that might answer the question of if these queens are also trans. While driving, Vida and Noxeema are giving Chi-Chi a hard time, asserting that she is not yet a full-fledged drag queen. Among other things, the elder queens say Chi-Chi is just a boy in a dress because she doesn't have the prerequisite street smarts. They make no mention of her foundation not matching her skin tone, which would've been my contention. Noxeema then goes into a bit of a monologue about identity:

"When a straight man puts on a dress and gets his sexual kicks, he is a transvestite. When a man is a woman trapped in a man's body and has the little operation, he is a transsexual. When a gay man has way too much fashion sense for one gender, he is a drag queen. And when a tired little Latin boy puts on a dress, he is simply a boy in a dress."

This moment of on-screen explication is particularly interesting considering that today, many years after the film's debut, Chi-Chi is canonically understood to be a baby trans woman. Candis Cayne, the famed trans drag performer who advised Swayze on his performance in *To Wong Foo*, is featured in the film's final scene, and went on to become the first openly trans actress to play a recurring trans character on primetime television in *Dirty Sexy Money*, said in 2020, "Chi-Chi was a trans icon, but she also showed us that gay men and trans women can both perform and work in drag side by side, and that those relationships are symbiotic."

Leguizamo, who was nominated for a Golden Globe for the role, commented, quite interestingly: "Drag didn't really exist in movies," he told *Today*. "There were straight men pretending to be women to get out of trouble or into trouble but this was not that. I was trying to make Chi-Chi a real-life trans character and Patty and Wesley were trying to be real drag queens."

But again, Chi-Chi's supposed transness, in terms of her identifying as a woman and not only a drag queen, is never explicitly articulated on-screen in the film, which was number one at the box office for two straight weeks upon its release. Reviews and press about it, and at least one summary in marketing materials, refer to the queens as "transvestites" and the film as another example of transvestism being "Hollywood's favorite form of safe sex, since its naughtiness is so toothless and lends itself to such happy platitudes," as a *New York Times* piece published Sept. 8, 1995 reads. But cross-dressing and drag alone does not a woman make.

And just in case it needs stating: While "transvestite" is defined as a person, usually a man, who dresses in clothes most often associated with, in binary terms, the opposite sex, the word has fallen out of major use and can be considered a slur. So . . . watch ya mouth!

This is, however, a stark difference between *To Wong Foo* and *The Adventures of Priscilla, Queen of the Desert*, the Oscar-winning Australian picture that premiered the year prior in 1994. Though both films are essentially about three drag queens on a road trip, one of the three queens in the Stephan Elliott–written and -directed comedy recognized in 1995 by the Academy for Lizzy Gardiner and Tim Chappel's costuming is a trans woman named Bernadette Bassenger, played by Terence Stamp. Stamp was perhaps most known at the time for his 1962 Oscar-nominated role in *Billy Budd*, and he starred in *Priscilla* opposite Hugo Weaving as Anthony "Tick" Belrose, whose drag persona is Mitzi Del Bra, and Guy Pearce as Adam Whitely, whose drag persona is Felicia Jollygoodfellow. The film, which helped usher in a new level of LGBTQ+ visibility for mainstream and queer audiences, follows the trio's journey from Sydney, Australia, to Alice Springs in a rickety tour bus they've named Priscilla. On their way to what will be a major performance in a resort town, their bus breaks down, forcing them to seek temporary refuge with, first, a welcoming group of First Nations peoples, then in a small town where—like in *To Wong Foo*—folks like them are not only an oddity but the objects of potential violence.

In this film, Bernadette *is* explicitly identified as a trans woman—the term "transsexual," which non-trans people also shouldn't say, was used in press materials and reviews. Though in the film's trailer, all three queens are referred to as "hard-working guys," textually there is never any question that she is trans. And when the queens are out of drag—something none of the other films show—we see both Tick and Adam as their boy selves when they're not performing, while Bernadette is just a more toned-down version of her drag persona and still a woman.

Three movies about drag queens. Three examples of on-screen narratives that are, based on text, subtext, or the power of the trans imagination, sites of trans possibilities in the '90s. Granted, there is a lot of what I like to call "problemasia" with all three of these films. Of course, my reading is more contemporary, and not necessarily reflective of the period-specific understandings of identity, or lack thereof, when they were made. But when you know better, you do better, so having robust and nuanced conversations about the many complexities of art of yesteryear with both an awareness of the sociocultural circumstances of when it was made alongside the lenses of today should only improve our discourse.

Priscilla uses deadnaming as a comedic and tritely vindictive storytelling device, and Bernadette's closest friends are the perpetrators of such violence. The film also features a tertiary Filipina character named Cynthia, whom Melba Marginson of the Centre for Filipino Concerns described at the time as "a gold-digger, a prostitute, an entertainer whose expertise is popping out ping-pong balls from her sex-organ, a manic depressive, loud and vulgar. The worst stereotype of the Filipina."

Marginson continued: "While all the main and secondary characters in the film were treated with respect, humanised and dignified, the Filipina was treated with condemnation, dehumanised and stripped of any form of dignity."

To Wong Foo is gender essentialist, because some women do, indeed, have penises. Some women do, also, "look like men"—and not because they're trans but because gender is a made-up social construct that ignores the lived reality of millions whose phenotypic traits, and the genotypic ones, too, don't squarely fit the presumed binary. I'm talking about women with chin hair. Men with button noses and soft jaw-lines. People of all genders with both broad shoulders and dainty hands and feet. I'm not one of them, but they do exist! Shout-out to the masculinely femme and femininely masc folks.

In *Midnight in the Garden of Good and Evil*, Chablis is a trifecta of the sassy Black diva, scary Black man, and jezebel tropes all in one, no matter how true to life the character might be to The Doll. And Minerva, the voodoo practitioner played by the legendary Irma P. Hall who is enlisted to help spiritually guide the defendant in the movie's court case, is a literal magical negro. And not in a #BlackGirlMagic sort of way.

Luckily, projects of yesteryear can be deemed problematic and still regarded for their cultural impact. It just is what it is. Because yet still, all three of these films that feature drag characters are important sites of early trans representation, and we must account for the ways trans people have seen slivers of ourselves at various points of our gender journeys in these types of characters.

But how do we make sense of these instances of both

potentially perceived and explicitly described transness on-screen in drag characters before we collectively had the language to describe it as such? The cultural lore surrounding these films, and the now-canonized reframing of what may have just been seen as drag characters (save Bernadette) has helped shift the conversation surrounding these pictures. These films were also mainstream successes in a lot of ways, like *Rent*, which consistently is a subject of discussion regarding if the character Angel Dumott Schunard, originated on Broadway and played in the 2005 film adaptation by Wilson Jermaine Heredia, is trans or not.

But what about smaller productions, like *Holiday Heart*, the cable movie directed by the legendary Robert Townsend in 2000 that starred Ving Rhames and Alfre Woodard? Rhames plays Holiday, a soft-hearted Black drag queen who takes in Woodard's drug-addicted single-mother character and her daughter in the aftermath of his boyfriend's death. In my experience, particularly when I'm talking with Black people about early images of trans representation, *Holiday* is invariably brought up. The thought is that if *Holiday Heart* was written today, the character might be trans considering how femme he was out of drag. I always have to admit a particular affinity I have for Rhames's portrayal. In many ways, it was yet another for me in my gender journey.

Or Patrik-Ian Polk's debut film, *Punks*, also from 2000. An exploration of Black gay life and friendship that would serve as foundational inspiration for *Noah's Arc* years later, it starred four friends in Los Angeles: a shy, virginal photographer in Seth Gilliam's Marcus; the outgoing Lothario Hill, played by Dwight Ewell; a hot-to-trot rich kid newbie in Renoly Santiago's Dante; and Jazzmun Nichcala Crayton's fabulous drag diva Crystal, also known as Chris. I never forgot about Crystal, her persisting slayage pulling my attention every time she was on-screen. So much so that when I was assigned to cover the Pan African Film Festival in 2015 by my *LA Times* editor and discovered that Jazzmun was a producer and star of the documentary *In Full Bloom: Transcending Gender* premiering at the fest, I spotlighted her and the movie with a feature. After *Punks*, Jazzmun went on to play all kinds of sex workers, the types of roles trans women have historically been forced to do, from *The 40-Year-Old Virgin* to *CSI: NY.* In 2017, she played real-life trans activist and minister Bobbi Jean Baker in ABC's miniseries *When We Rise*, a retelling of the gay rights movement in the United States, starting with the Stonewall riots of 1969.

I think it's important to extend trans representation to include some of the drag characters I've mentioned in this chapter, and not just as a project that attempts to bolster or superficially fill out our history. So much of the assumed canon includes no people of color, and that's due to the ways white trans people, white trans women in particular, were afforded varying levels of visibility because of their ability to embody a certain type of white personhood. But swirling around and in every film and television show is the sociopolitical environment in which it was created. By including some of these drag characters in this conversation, especially Black ones and others of color, we recognize the limitations of our visual culture, which is necessarily influenced by trans-erasive realities.

━━

A conversation about drag, especially in film, TV, and broader pop culture, is never complete without not only considering but centering the San Diego–born cultural icon known simply by his first name: RuPaul. To quote one Nicki Minaj, whose aesthetic can be said to mirror that of some Black femme queens: All these bitches is her sons, and daughters and kids. Regretfully, the core of my awareness of RuPaul seems to only go back as far as season 1 of *RuPaul's Drag Race*, the titan of a reality competition show that thrust a once-taboo art of expression solidly into the mainstream. Charge it to my head and not my heart. Because I know, without a doubt, that I definitely came across her charisma, uniqueness, nerve, and talent before the franchise sashayed its way onto its original broadcaster Logo TV in 2009. That was my senior year of high school, when I was copresident of my school's award-winning Model United Nations team, on the school newspaper and student government, and a member of the Tree Huggers club with my girlfriend, her bestie, and our crew. I'm certain we knew who RuPaul was, but I have no specific memories, save a 1995 episode of *Sister, Sister* in which RuPaul plays a boutique owner that Jackée Harry's Lisa, a designer and seamstress, is trying to convince to buy her original fashions. But I likely didn't see it until at least five years later, in syndication.

But before that and before she became "the world's most famous and influential drag performer," as a 2017 *Entertainment Weekly* feature describes her, Ru was a punk rocker and rock 'n' roller, drag being an onstage "ruse," he said to Terry Gross on NPR's *Fresh Air* in 2020 about his genderfuck era of performance. "We did drag as a social commentary. It was a reaction to the Reagan '80s. And it wasn't trying to look real or pass; it was a rebellion against the status quo. . . . We did drag, but we did drag as a punk rock statement."

Fenton Bailey, one of the founders of *Drag Race* production company World of Wonder and a longtime friend of RuPaul, recalled first meeting her during a music conference held at the Marriott Marquis in New York's Times Square in the mid-'80s. "Ru was in that incredible lobby in thigh-high wader boots, jockstrap, shoulder pads, and shredded bin liner, waving his album and a big red wig," he told *Vanity Fair* in a 2019 cover story of RuPaul, photographed by Annie Leibovitz. The cover line reads, "Happy Ru Year! It's RuPaul's world and you're lucky to live in it," largely in all caps.

When Ru realized that he could make the money he needed and wanted by changing his style of drag, he did just that, putting away the subversiveness of androgyny and going high glam. "The way to make money was go-go dancing, to host different club nights. So I decided, you know what? I'm going to shave my legs. I'm going to shave my chest. And I'm going to roll some socks tightly into a bra, and I'm going to go out there and look like a *Soul Train* dancer," he said in the *Fresh Air* interview. And because she just knew that to be a commercial success and be mainstream she needed to be nonthreatening to middle America—or Betty and Joe Beer Can, as Ru says—she developed a recipe for success that became the blonde-wigged glamazon we know today, one that removed the subversive sexuality that other queens who'd come before her embraced:

"My present drag persona was developed out of my study of pop culture and how to create a caricature that someone could draw on the page and be recognizable," RuPaul told *Vanity Fair* in a video interview accompanying the 2019 cover. The persona's name is Monster, though Muva would likely do just fine. "I took two parts Cher, three parts Diana Ross, a dash of Dolly Parton and a little bit of David Bowie and James Brown . . . and a smathering of Bugs Bunny and that's how my public persona came to be."

Enlisting the support of the community of artists and creatives around her, this new persona gave way to "Supermodel

RuPaul

(You Better Work)," Ru's 1992 track that peaked at number forty-five on the *Billboard* Hot 100 and number two on the *Billboard* Hot Dance Music/Club Play chart. It became an anthem worthy of a place on a 2017 *Buzzfeed* list of "the 101 Greatest Dance Songs of the '90s" and a 2018 *Pitchfork* list of the fifty songs that defined the previous fifty years of Pride, and it catapulted Ru and drag into the mainstream.

In 1994, RuPaul made her big-screen debut in Spike Lee's seventh film, *Crooklyn*, a semiautobiographical tale about a Brooklyn schoolteacher, her stubborn and naive jazz musician husband, and their five kids, cowritten by Spike and his siblings Joie and Cinqué. The film starred one of the best actors of any time and any gender, Alfre Woodard, alongside Delroy Lindo, and RuPaul played "Bodega Woman," a customer who dances with another at the local bodega to the awe of a young Black child looking on. That same year, she became the face of MAC Cosmetics, the first drag queen to secure a major beauty contract.

A year later, in addition to *Sister, Sister,* Ru made a cameo in *To Wong Foo* and *The Brady Bunch Movie*, and by 1996, her star power was solidified in the form of the release of her autobiography, *Lettin' It All Hang Out,* the year prior and *The RuPaul Show*, a VH1 talk show that ran for only one hundred episodes but managed to book everyone from Diana Ross to Bernadette Peters, Duran Duran to the Queen of Hip-Hop Soul, Mary J. Blige. *RPDR* judge Michelle Visage was Ru's cohost on the talk show, which was also one of the first national television programs in the United States hosted by an openly gay person. For clarity here, I'm talking about Ru, who, if you don't know, is a cis gay man. I use he/him and she/her pronouns interchangeably for Ru, who, on the subject of pronouns, once said: "You can call me he. You can call me she. You can call me Regis and Kathie Lee; I don't care! Just as long as you call me."

Journalist Richard Lawson, author of the *Vanity Fair* story, described the importance of RuPaul having a talk show: "The startle of RuPaul's unapologetic pose attaining such a prominent position on major airwaves enshrined the Monster as an emblem—perhaps *the* emblem, both inviting and defiant—of modern drag."

Invariably, RuPaul's visibility in the mainstream, which has only increased in the last two decades, has catalyzed cultural conversations about identity, gender, and sexuality. There are surely plenty of academic papers from here to Cameroon that take a look at how Ru and drag's mainstreamification—assuming drag, especially the styles of drag that truly get a hometown club up off its feet, can ever really be mainstream—has dovetailed with cultural discourse around trans visibility, and the conflation therein. But I think the most obvious illustration of the relationship between drag on-screen and some trans people coming into themselves lies in the contestants of *RuPaul's Drag Race*.

There are now countless queens who've competed on the show as trans people, evidence of and further concretizing the ongoing relationship between drag and trans possibilities. Kylie Sonique Love was the first person in show history to come out as trans, which she did during the season 2 reunion; she says the producers knew she was trans when they cast her, though she hadn't publicly transitioned at the time. Kylie eventually became the first openly trans woman to win an American version of the reality competition show, in 2021, when she returned for and won season 6 of *RuPaul's Drag Race: All Stars*. Angele Anang, who won the second season of *Thailand's Drag Race* in 2019, was the first openly trans winner in the entire franchise.

Also add to the list Monica Beverly Hillz, who came out while filming season 5; Peppermint, who was runner-up of season 9; and queens like Gia Gunn, Jiggly Caliente, Carmen

Carrera, Laganja Estranja, and more who came out as trans after their (first, for some) time on the show. In 2021, on the thirteenth season of the series, Gottmik became the first out trans man to compete, and he was followed in 2022 by five transfeminine people on the show. Fans nicknamed queen Kerri Colby "Tranos," like Marvel's Thanos, because of the role she played in inspiring and supporting the transitions of castmates Kornbread "The Snack" Jeté, Bosco, Jasmine Kennedie, and Willow Pill, who won season 14, before, during, and/or after the show.

That said, RuPaul and *Drag Race*'s herstory as it relates to trans issues isn't all hunky-dory. It bears mentioning that Ru, in a 2018 *Guardian* interview, said that it was unlikely that a trans woman would be cast on the show. "You can identify as a woman and say you're transitioning, but it changes once you start changing your body," he said. This transphobic comment was made a year after the show was widely acclaimed for featuring Peppermint as its first openly trans contestant; she had publicly identified as trans before being cast on the show but had not medically transitioned. The backlash was immediate. Ru sorta kinda apologized, tweeting: "I understand and regret the hurt I have caused. The trans community are heroes of our shared LGBTQ movement. You are my teachers."

But this wasn't his first time saying something deeply problematic regarding transness. When NSYNCer Lance Bass had to apologize for using the slur "tranny" in 2012, saying he thought it was okay to use because *Drag Race* used it, Ru was openly annoyed. Ru even asserted, wrongly, that "no one has ever said the word 'tranny' in a derogatory sense." Then two years later, the show's network ditched, for season 7 and all those after, the "You've got she-mail!" sound that would precede RuPaul's workroom entrance each episode—because the term "she-mail" was a play on "she-male," a slur directed at trans women to delegitimize their identities. Discussing this decision in 2016, Ru, again, put her foot in her mouth. "We do take feelings seriously and intention seriously, and the intention is not to be hateful at all," he told *Vulture*'s E. Alex Jung. "But if you are trigger-happy and you're looking for a reason to reinforce your own victimhood, your own perception of yourself as a victim, you'll look for anything that will reinforce that."

Interestingly enough, today, it's totally possible, and likely, that someone's first image of a trans person in popular culture is one of the queens on *RuPaul's Drag Race*. And I think that's wonderful.

━━

At one time, *Noah's Arc* and André Leon Talley and Miss J on *America's Next Top Model* were the wind in my sails that helped push me along my journey. But was what I was seeing on-screen really me? Or did they just show me slivers of myself at the time, my fullness still never actually reflected?

As folks from communities that have been historically excluded—Black and Brown, queer and trans, disabled, etc.— we're used to seeing ourselves in actors and the characters they play. Growing up in a world that privileges and centers certain identities over others, it's common for us to water down the representation we actually needed or wanted, having accepted stand-in possibility models that only speak to one aspect of our complex, multifaceted identities. Though I'm confident many of us don't even recognize the ways that our go-to touchpoints truly don't hold *all* of us, I also have to recognize it as the skill of survival that it is. Sometimes it's easier, and necessary, to just say that Elle Woods in *Legally*

Blonde made me want to be a lawyer even though I'm not a white, cishet blonde from Bel-Air. Sometimes it's more advantageous to say *A Different World* made me want to go to a Black college, even though the show seemed to never address queerness, or transness for that matter, therefore forecasting, in some ways, what would be a challenging experience for me as a student coming into themself on the campus of Morehouse College. The reality is that many of us have settled for inadequate, monofaceted, incomplete representation. Like my ancestors, we took the crumbs and the spoils and turned them into feasts, fashioning a cornucopia of possibilities we didn't *really* know was possible. We could dream, though, and that was motivation enough.

This is all to say that "When was the first time you saw yourself on-screen?" is a scam of a question. It wrongly presupposes that we all have seen ourselves reflected in media, especially in a positive light. But many of us haven't. Let it also be known that this question treats our identities as human beings as finite, as if the people we were told we were when we were younger are the same individuals we are in adulthood. As if our beings don't shift and change like seasons, or like a mother's level of patience the second time she asks her child to clean their room. And though we may forever carry within us a younger self who once felt represented, it is also true that the person we are today deserves to be seen, too. Is representation still representation even if it only reflected the fullness of our lives when we were younger and more impressionable? What, then, does it mean to see ourselves?

The best forms of representation are those that hold us, and hold us the longest. I've sometimes felt most held by images of Black drag queens—from that one episode of *Noah's Arc* when Rodney Chester's Alex slays a lip sync of Brainstorm's

1977 jam "Lovin' Is Really My Game" in drag for the first time with his crew behind him to *RuPaul's Drag Race*'s BeBe Zahara Benet and Latrice Royale. And not because I wanted to be them, but because I wanted and want to be a self who recognizes gender as the scam it is and dares to play in its face on the daily.

A better question than "When was the first time you saw yourself on-screen?" is "What depiction on-screen has held you the best, the longest?" "Do you feel held, in your fullness, by what's on-screen now?"

Otherwise, we'll keep asking people about the first time the media showed them how to be palatable to the masses, and we'll keep getting responses that reproduce respectability and collapse our complexities.

VIEWING GUIDE

THE QUEEN (1968)

Directed by Frank Simon and narrated by Flawless Sabrina, this doc depicts the experiences of the drag queens organizing and participating in the 1967 Miss All-America Camp Beauty Pageant. Among the contestants is Crystal LaBeija, who would go on to form the influential House of LaBeija featured in *Paris Is Burning*.

THE ADVENTURES OF PRISCILLA, QUEEN OF THE DESERT (1994)

Three drag queens—two gay men and a trans woman—take their acts on the road, driving across the Australian desert in a bus they've named Priscilla. Along the way, they encounter both enthusiastic crowds and homophobes as their show and friendship is tested.

TO WONG FOO, THANKS FOR EVERYTHING! JULIE NEWMAR (1995)

Wesley Snipes, Patrick Swayze, and John Leguizamo play three drag queens driving cross-country from New York to Los Angeles for a major drag competition. But when their car breaks down, they end up stranded in a small, conservative town.

MIDNIGHT IN THE GARDEN OF GOOD AND EVIL (1997)

Based on John Berendt's 1994 book of the same name, come for the mystery thriller, stay to see The Lady Chablis steal every scene she's in.

CHAPTER
3

REALITY BITES

ONE OF THE FIRST TRANS-IDENTIFIED PEOPLE I SAW ON TELEVISION WAS ISIS KING. It was the fall of 2008, my senior year of high school, when the *America's Next Top Model* craze was in its prime. A devoted fan, I've watched every single episode—even when the show jumped the shark—since the beginning. This was the eleventh "cycle"; true fans know that *ANTM* didn't have seasons. I remember the first time I saw her.

Well, the first-first time was a year earlier, during the tenth cycle. For the contestants' first photoshoot of the competition, they were challenged to make homelessness fashionable. Posing in a back alleyway, accompanied by real people navigating houselessness, the shoot was theoretically supposed to raise awareness about homeless youth. It was, according to Tyra Banks, inspired by a segment she did on her talk show where she lived as a homeless person (with cameras following her) for a day. In the shoot, the model contestants were dressed in homeless drag, or street clothes, while the actual folks experiencing houselessness donned high-fashion wares.

One of the houseless extras was Isis, who had heard about the opportunity to participate in this photoshoot while a client at New York's Ali Forney Center. Named after Ali Forney, a Black trans health advocate, sex worker, and peer educator whose 1997 murder has never been solved, the Ali Forney Center is one of the largest LGBTQ community centers helping queer and trans homeless youth in the United States.

As soon as the first contestant gets on set for her round of shots, we hear photo-shoot creative director Mr. Jay raving about Isis's performance in the background. "Isis is wearing me out down on the mattress," he says, peering into a monitor. And Isis was serving! In every shot where the camera was largely focused on the competing model, Isis's fierce bone structure and modelesque allure, which had been crafted as a member of the ball scene, stole attention.

After the shoot, Isis pulled Mr. Jay to the side, she said in an *Us* magazine interview. "If I wanted to come back and try out for the show, have you ever had a girl who was born in the wrong body?" she says she asked him.

At the start of the eleventh cycle of the show, Isis is one of the featured semifinalists who is brought in front of a panel that includes Mr. Jay, Miss J, and Tyra herself. At this early stage in the competition, contestants have to impress these three to make it to the final group of women who will actually compete. Mr. Jay is the first to bring up Isis's performance from the homeless shelter photo shoot, to which Tyra responds:

"It blew me away, and I tell my staff, I'm like, 'This girl is absolutely amazing. She's gotta come back for *America's Next Top Model*.'" As she says this, a smirk forms in the corner of her mouth. "I said, 'This girl . . .' and my staff said, 'Tyra, there's something a little different about that girl.'"

Isis then proceeds to disclose that she was "born physically male, but mentally, everything else, I was born female." The show cuts to a confessional in which Isis further details her gender journey: "Some people might say that I'm transgender. Some people might say transsexual," she says with an eye roll. "Personally, I prefer 'born in the wrong body.'"

I was fascinated. Not in the gross, invasive ways most folks are when trans people discuss our truths; I was fascinated by the language usage. "Born in the wrong body" was so simple yet so accurate, I imagined, and it awakened something within me. Like that first burst of fairy-godmother dust in *Cinderella* that jump-starts her imagination and belief in the impossible. (I'm obviously talking about the Black *Cinderella* starring icons on icons—Brandy Norwood, Whitney Houston, Whoopi Goldberg, the late Natalie Desselle Reid, and more.) At that moment, Isis became my favorite contestant, even before she started modeling.

A quick note here: "born in the wrong body" is absolutely *not* the preferred language to use in discussing trans people's gender journeys. For all the cis-sies, don't let me catch you out here using phrases like this! Today, we recognize it as a limiting trope.

Back to *ANTM*! As the scene continues, Tyra employs what we now all agree, but many people also believed at the time, was an invasive line of questioning. She wanted to know if Isis had had bottom surgery, which she hadn't but did desire. I remember thinking, even as just a high school senior, "Who cares?"

After Isis leaves the judges and is back in the pen with the other contestants, a group of women are talking about having small chests. One of them, a fellow Black woman, remarks about Isis's. In a confessional, she says, "Isis, I thought she looked a little manly. Like I have small boobs, too, but her boobs—she has no boobs."

The show then cuts back to the model pen and follows this woman who beckons Isis into the "itty-bitty committee." But Isis already knows what's going on. We always do. After disclosing her gender journey, most of the other contestants immaturely gawk or giggle. In a confessional, the woman who couldn't mind her business says, "Ain't this supposed to be a girl competition? Like, how did you get through the door?"

In another confessional, a white nineteen-year-old from Pawleys Island, SC—not a three-hour drive from the very city in which I watched the show—says, "If I have to get along with Isis, I will. But then again, if it comes between me and my goal, I'll stomp that man right out the competition." I wanted to beat her ass. I still do. Only one other model is shown in the episode taking up for Isis.

Isis went on to become one of the fourteen finalists that year, but she was eliminated rather early. On the cycle's fifth episode, the photo-shoot challenge required the models to pose with their faces partially underwater in a pool. Isis struggled, seemingly insecure about having to wear a bathing suit. She was eliminated that week, placing tenth. I was so sad, and disappointed. Having watched all ten cycles up to that point, I thought Isis had everything to win the show.

When she returned for cycle 17, the series' first All Stars season, I was pumped. Despite the shit she faced the first go-round, I interpreted her return as a fierce desire to win. At this stage in her journey, she'd had bottom surgery, financed by Tyra Banks's talk show, and so she was clear that some of the challenges she had faced in cycle 11—lack of confidence, body insecurities, etc.—were no longer concerns. But due to an unfortunate twist in the game, Isis was eliminated in the third episode. The ladies were split into two teams for a challenge where they had to answer questions in an interview. Isis's team lost, and immunity was given to the winners. Isis landed in the bottom two, but not because her photo was even close to the worst of the bunch. The worst photos were of models who had immunity. She placed thirteenth.

Revisiting articles published by mainstream press during her first *ANTM* stint, I can only imagine the intense pressure Isis felt. One article dated September 23, 2008, and written by the Associated Press, deadnames her multiple times, and in the first sentence, no less. "As a little boy in the Washington suburbs, [redacted] liked to pretend to be Lil' Kim or a Pink Power Ranger," it begins.

We don't give Isis enough credit.

We also don't give Leiomy Maldonado enough credit, the Afro-Puerto Rican, Bronx-born "Wonder Woman of Vogue." Because before she was featured in Willow Smith's moment-defining "Whip My Hair" music video in 2010 and before she became the most important judge on HBO Max's ballroom competition show *Legendary* ten years later, the iconic dancer was *being* judged on *America's Best Dance Crew*.

A competition show à la *So You Think You Can Dance* but for groups, MTV's *America's Best Dance Crew* gave dance crews the chance to win $100,000. Former NSYNCer JC Chasez, rapper Lil Mama, and choreographer Shane Sparks were the judges for the first four seasons of the series, produced by record producer and former *American Idol* judge Randy Jackson. On the fourth season, which aired in 2009, Leiomy made history as the first openly trans woman to compete on the show. She was a member of the troupe Vogue Evolution, alongside Dashaun Wesley, who'd become the host and emcee of *Legendary*, Devon Webster (aka Pony), Malechi Williams, and Jorel Rios (aka Prince), and together, they reintroduced the world to voguing, the dance style that came out of New York's ballroom scene, for whom most folks' reference points were either *Paris Is Burning* or Madonna's 1990 song "Vogue."

But even before Leiomy and her team hit the *ABDC* stage, the artist-athlete's impact on dance and culture had already been felt. An all-female group from the show's first season, Fysh N Chicks, had incorporated one of Leiomy's signature moves into their challenge during week two of season 1, which aired early 2008. The move, which is essentially a hair flip but with a little razzle-dazzle, is known as "the lolly."

About the group's decision to do the show themselves, Leiomy told me for *Zora* magazine, "Around that time, there were videos circulating of different artists having people *try* to vogue in their music videos. For us, it was like, if we have this chance to go on TV and show the world where voguing comes from, and to let them know that it's a real art form, a real dance form, why not?"

Vogue Evolution was eliminated in the fifth episode, but not before Leiomy, who had first discovered voguing at Kips Bay Boys and Girls Club and honed her skills watching VHS tapes of other trans women voguing, namely the late Yolanda Jourdan and Alloura Jourdan Zion, had to deal with judge Lil Mama questioning her womanhood in front of the whole world. In a recap of the previous week on episode 4, Leiomy is shown expressing frustration and abruptly leaving Vogue Evolution's dress rehearsal. In a confessional, she says that the only thing keeping her in the competition is her community, the fact that being on the show had made her "the face of transgender" and she wanted her fans to not be disappointed.

Lil Mama called her behavior "unacceptable," adding, "You always have to remember your truth. You were born a man, and you are becoming a woman. If you're going to become a woman, act like a lady. Don't be a bird. . . . Even though you're the face for transgenders, you're the face for America right now with this group and it's not about anybody else."

Besides the cringe use of "transgender" as a noun—it's fine, everybody was doing it back then—the gender stereotypes perpetuated by Lil Mama's comments angered many in the trans and queer community. She was basically saying that in order to be the woman Leiomy knew herself to be, she had to carry herself in a way that didn't remind people of her sex assigned at birth—because anger and frustration are apparently emotions reserved for men? GLAAD received a number of calls and emails about the incident, prompting them to reach out to Lil Mama, who then "clarified" her commentary in a statement that read, in part, "My remarks were never meant to be disrespectful regarding Leiomy's gender nor offensive to the LGBT community. . . . However, in hindsight, I recognize that my words may have come across as hurtful."

I highlight both Isis King and Leiomy Maldonado for two reasons. One, their reality TV contributions to trans visibility, and especially that of Black trans women, aren't talked about enough for me. It's my belief that every time we stroll down memory lane of how we, as a trans community, got to where we are, we must acknowledge the women and men and people who at one time charted new territory—territory that eventually led to, for example, *Project Runway* featuring Mimi Tao and DD Smith as its first trans and nonbinary models, respectively, in 2019, or the casting of Jayla Sullivan as a dancer on Lizzo's *Watch Out for the Big Grrrls* in 2022. We don't get these more recent inroads of inclusion, ones where these folks *aren't* the recipients of on-camera transphobic foolishness, without Isis and Leiomy, and women like Jaila Simms, who in 2009 competed on MTV's *Making His Band*. While Diddy searched for folks to join him onstage as backup singers, Jaila had to navigate through everyone involved reminding one another and themselves that she was assigned male at birth every step of the way.

But I also spotlight these women because of the composure and resilience they had to display in the face of ignorance. With so many eyes on them, they had to smile and grin, like Cassi Davis as Ella in *Madea Goes to Jail*, as they were misgendered and questioned and otherwise invalidated. Trans folks, and others from historically marginalized and excluded communities, are always expected to be so grateful at the mere fact that we're invited to the party, because the invitation alone is such a huge move for the entities welcoming us in. But we're not supposed to call them out for how their work of inclusion doesn't start and end with an invite. We're not supposed to express our disappointment and frustration and anger when the environments we're in show their true colors regarding how they feel about the complexity of our truths, or at least not in ways that'll disrupt goings-on they'd rather not disrupt.

Perhaps that expectation is changing. Regardless, the world is lucky trans people naturally have resilient spirits. But also, why we always gotta be resilient?

■

There was a tie for the 2009 GLAAD Media Award for Outstanding Reality Program. I'll talk about *I Want to Work for Diddy*, which introduced us to a pre–*Orange Is the New Black* Laverne Cox in the next chapter, but that show shared the honor with *Transamerican Love Story*, the *Bachelor*-style dating show that was the first in the United States on which contestants competed for the attention and approval of a transgender woman, Calpernia Addams. With the help of her friend and producing partner Andrea James and host Alec Mapa, she weeded through eight men on the show, including Jim Howley, who is also trans.

At the time, most people knew Calpernia for a tragic situation that occurred almost a decade earlier. In the late '90s, she began dating Barry Winchell, an infantry soldier in the Army. When word of their relationship spread to Winchell's fellow soldiers, he was harassed and ultimately murdered. His killing and the trial that followed garnered widespread media attention and a formal, President Bill Clinton–ordered review of the problematic "Don't Ask, Don't Tell" military policy in place at the time. The 2003 film *Soldier's Girl* tells this story. Addams was played by cis actor Lee Pace and Winchell by Troy Garity, Jane Fonda's son.

So Calpernia knew intimately the stakes of a show where men who were "open to dating trans women," as it was described at the time, vied for her love. "The amazing thing that Logo did with this was they showed trans people dating as being so normal, like it really is," Addams told the *Los Angeles Daily News'* Greg Hernandez in 2008. Hernandez ran the outlet's queer blog *Out in Hollywood*, believed to be the first queer blog of its type at a major daily newspaper in the US. "I think it's going to open it up for trans women to feel worthy of love and for guys to not be afraid to date us."

James added: "We often get portrayed as so tragic and serious. This was just a chance to have some fun."

Transamerican Love Story was ahead of its time. A look at some of the press headlines of the time tell the story. Perez Hilton's blog, which at the time dealt in seedy, salacious gossip, read "The Bachelorette (That Used To Be A Bachelor)." A 2007 *ABC News* article read "Guy Turned Girl Seeks Love on Reality TV." Almost sixty years after Christine Jorgensen was referred to on the cover of the *New York Daily News* with the headline "Ex-GI Becomes Blonde Beauty."

"One of the most important things to me about this project was that the guys knew everything up front," Addams told

ABC News. "I never want to feel like I'm deceiving someone about my past. My history does carry a lot of weight for a lot of people."

This comment is an interesting one, considering the lesser-known reality TV predecessor to *Transamerican Love Story*, *There's Something About Miriam*. Another incarnation of a *Bachelor*-style show, *There's Something About Miriam*, which originally aired in the United Kingdom in 2004, followed six men trying to win the love of Miriam Rivera, a twenty-one-year-old Mexico-born model who lived in New York City, and £10,000. The show, however, was based on what many might call deception, as the gentlemen callers were not told that Miriam was trans until the final episode of the Ibiza-shot experience—hence the "something" about Miriam.

I didn't know about Miriam or her show until 2021, when the Trace Lysette–hosted podcast *Harsh Reality: The Story of Miriam Rivera* was released. Produced by Wondery in partnership with Imara Jones's TransLash Media, a trans journalism and personal narrative project committed to telling trans stories to save trans lives, the gripping six-episode investigative series details how Miriam went from being one of the girls to the first openly trans person of any race to star in a reality television show in the world. A peek behind the salacious headlines of the time—when word got out about how Miriam and the show purposefully didn't disclose her gender history, the guys collectively filed a personal injury lawsuit, which delayed the airing of the show by a year; the press was rabid upon the show's final airing—the podcast humanizes Miriam by interviewing trans people who knew her.

"Like many trans women from the '90s era and before, Miriam was a woman ahead of her time; a diamond in the rough that the world couldn't appreciate in the way she deserved," Lysette said in a press release at the time. "I had the pleasure of knowing Miriam through NYC nightlife and the ballroom scene. She was a part of the House of Xtravaganza when I was earning my stripes in the House of Angel in the early 00s. She was always kind to me and I feel honored to help bring this podcast about her life to the listeners. I hope she can finally be celebrated and appreciated for the pioneer that she was."

And a pioneer she was! Despite her knowing role in the setup of the show, Miriam was making a case that trans women deserve to be loved, out loud, long before words like "trans-attracted" or "trans-amorous" became part of the latest social-media hot take. She desired love, and fame, and sought out both in that unabashed way that trans people, especially trans women and femmes, are forced to navigate an inhospitable world. An attempt to do what Calpernia Addams and *Transamerican Love Story* did four years later, at least in Miriam's mind, *There's Something About Miriam* was also ahead of its time.

"The world was so far behind that they just didn't get how special we are," Lysette told *PinkNews*. "Unfortunately, the world is still behind. I still don't think that we're there. And that breaks my heart."

━━━

Since 2008, the first year that trans people were meaningfully represented in a number of reality shows, there's been a rather consistent presence of the community on people's TV screens. I'd venture to say that it is reality TV, not films and scripted genres, that accounts for most of the positive portrayals of trans folks, as the medium sometimes offers trans people greater agency. That said, I also recognize the ways reality TV producers sometimes manipulate people to create drama to meet a ratings demand. In fact, since the year that gave us *Transamerican Love Story*, Laverne Cox on *I Want to Work for Diddy*, and Isis King on *ANTM* through at least 2015, at least one show earning a nomination from GLAAD for Outstanding Reality Program each year featured a trans person. In 2015, there were nearly ten reality-based shows featuring at least one trans person that were eligible for recognition from the media-advocacy organization. All five of that year's nominees featured a trans person, mostly trans women: E!'s *I Am Cait*, which followed the coming out of former Olympian and Kardashian parent Caitlyn Jenner; TLC's *I Am Jazz,* about a then-teenage Jazz Jennings, who was first interviewed about being trans at age six by Barbara Walters; Discovery Life's *New Girls on the Block*, a doc series about six transgender women from Kansas City who formed a tightly knit friend group; Oxygen's *The Prancing Elites Project*, which followed the Mobile, Alabama, J-setting dance team, one of whose members was a trans woman, Timberly Smith; and Fuse's *Transcendent*, which centered on the personal and professional relationships of a group of transgender women who performed at AsiaSF, a San Francisco nightclub. *I Am Cait* and *I Am Jazz* tied that year. Nick Adams, GLAAD's longtime director of transgender media, called reality shows a "really bright spot in terms of trans people being able to see themselves on TV" to me around that time.

Much of the discourse about trans representation on reality television hyper-focuses on images of trans women. Many have pontificated about why this is so, and even scripted portrayals follow this model. Proposed reasons include everything from the supposed "passing privilege" that some trans men and transmasculine people have to our society's preoccupation with ogling and critiquing femininity in ways we don't masculinity. 2020's *Disclosure* details, in part, how the commodification of the female form contributes to this disparity.

Regardless of the reason, though, trans men—and non-binary people, though that is changing—have largely been invisible on television, GLAAD's associate director of transgender media Alex Schmider told *Time* in 2020. "Historically, I don't recall a time when there were more than two or three trans men on TV at the same time," he said.

Two trans men on reality television that, to me, most bear highlighting are Chaz Bono and Zeke Smith. Chaz Bono, the child of entertainers Sonny Bono and Cher, documented his transition in the film *Becoming Chaz*, which aired on the Oprah Winfrey Network in May 2011. In September of that year, he became the first openly trans man to star on a major network television show for something unrelated to being transgender, as a contestant on the thirteenth season of *Dancing with the Stars*. He was also the first trans person to compete on the show. Though he did not win, his casting and performance on the show was a huge moment in visibility for trans people, especially transmasculine folks.

The next major moment—after the equally important casting of Tyler Ford in season 2 of *The Glee Project* and Dennis Starr in AMC's *Small Town Security*—came in 2017 with Zeke Smith on the thirty-fourth season of the competition show *Survivor*. On *Survivor*, a show that takes a group of strangers and places them on an isolated island where they must provide food, fire, and shelter for themselves, contestants compete in challenges, voting to eliminate someone every week until a sole survivor wins a cash prize. On this season of the show, subtitled *Game Changers—Mamanuca Islands*, which marked Zeke's second appearance on *Survivor*, a fellow contestant outed Zeke as transgender to the other castmates in an attempt to paint Zeke as deceitful for not disclosing. Upon the episode's airing, Zeke said years later that he "went from someone who very few people knew to be trans to one of the most visible transgender men in the world" almost instantly. What's remarkable, though, was the immediate rebuke and outrage expressed by Zeke's castmates and host Jeff Probst.

Between the episode's taping and airing, CBS worked with Zeke and GLAAD to craft an approach of how to best handle the episode. Timed to its release, Zeke penned an op-ed in the *Hollywood Reporter* reflecting on why he didn't disclose his gender journey—"I wanted the show to desire me as a game player and an eccentric storyteller, not as 'The First Trans *Survivor* Player.'" He also called out his former castmate for invoking "one of the most odious stereotypes

Zeke Smith, Yance Ford, Tre'Vell, and Marquise Vilson

of transgender people, a stereotype that is often used as an excuse for violence and even murder. In proclaiming 'Zeke is not the guy you think he is' and that 'there is deception on levels y'all don't understand,' Varner is saying that I'm not really a man and that simply living as my authentic self is a nefarious trick. In reality, by being Zeke the dude, I am being my most honest self—as is every other transgender person going about their daily lives."

There were nine months between the filming and airing of that season of *Survivor*. I must admit, I was never very into the show. I had watched a number of the early and middle seasons, but the Black folks—because I've been rooting for everybody Black since I was in utero, honey—never seemed to make it far enough in the competition, save a few instances. The way racial politics played out, even for the non-Black folks of color, always felt off to me. So, when I started getting emails while working at the *Los Angeles Times* about this major moment that was about to happen on television, I was intrigued. I didn't watch live, but the next morning, Zeke's name and reactions to the outing were all over social media and every outlet. Much like Zeke told the *Hollywood Reporter* later, I was surprised at how overwhelmingly positive the reaction was: "I was prepared for salacious headlines and dredged-up photos from my past," Zeke said. "I was prepared to be re-victimized. That the outrage was all toward the wrongdoer and the sympathy was towards me . . . It was a unique moment in the way trans people are handled in the public eye."

This was a moment where it felt like things were changing before my eyes, too. While this was obviously after the infamous "transgender tipping point," it wasn't clear to me until the reporting on Zeke's story that culture at large was also beginning to reject the age-old, stereotypical narratives around trans people who don't disclose their gender journeys.

I remember being in awe of how gentle and compassionate so much of mainstream media and other popular discourse was toward Zeke. And while TV and culture critics debated whether or not CBS should've aired the episode in the first place, Zeke was never made out to be the villain.

Then again, Zeke was a man, a white one at that. How might the reactions have been different, by fellow competitors, Jeff Probst, and the broader community, if Zeke was a Black trans woman? If it was *The Bachelor* instead of *Survivor*? Actually, I think we know the answer.

———

In April 2019, I received an email from a publicist about the Ava DuVernay–directed limited series about the now-described Exonerated Five *When They See Us*. A recounting of the real-life miscarriage of justice that was the 1989 Central Park Five case, the four-episode film starred the likes of Jharrel Jerome, Niecy Nash, Blair Underwood, Aunjanue Ellis, Marsha Stephanie Blake, Famke Janssen, and more. The email invited me to a marathon screening of all four episodes at Netflix's headquarters in Hollywood. Knowing the impact *When They See Us* was projected to have on the culture, I jumped at the opportunity.

If you haven't yet seen it, you must. It's a tough watch, and I've only ever made it through the four episodes in full once. But I remember that first time. I was already emotionally raw from the first three episodes. Angered by the way those kids were treated by the system, which was heightened because of the outsized role Donald Trump, who was president at the time the series was premiering, had played in the media firestorm that was this case, I wasn't sure I could make it through the last episode. The one thing that kept me going was knowing the real-life outcome that would invariably be depicted at the end. So, I persisted. And then Isis King came on the screen.

In the series, she plays Marci, the older sibling of Jerome's Korey Wise, who, of the five Black and Brown boys wrongfully convicted of raping a white woman, was the oldest at sixteen years old and was sentenced to adult prison. The majority of Wise's fourteen-year sentence was spent in solitary confinement. Marci, who was close with Wise and was trans, died while Wise was imprisoned.

Surely there was little way to know that Korey had a trans sibling; much of the case and the lore surrounding it hyper-focused on the injustice of their treatment and sentences. To that end, Ava DuVernay didn't have to include Marci and her relationship to Korey in the film. And even if she did want to include it, there didn't need to be a full-on character, and not one played by a trans actress. To see a Black trans woman playing a Black trans woman in this Black-ass series written and directed by a Black cis woman—and then to see Isis, whose post-*ANTM* journey I'd witnessed, including a stint on the short-lived reality show *Strut*, a 2016 Oxygen series about a group of transgender models trying to make a name for themselves in the world of fashion, playing such a thoughtfully rendered character—it all undid me.

In reflection, there was so much already happening on the screen and in the series that to then see transness tangibly show up—because wherever there is Blackness we are there too, just usually not named, maybe on the periphery if physically present at all—was impactful, another moment that made me go "Wow . . . things really are changing." And then to witness Isis play Marci pre- and post-transition at a time when one of the leading reasons Hollywood creatives often said they didn't cast trans people to play trans characters was because they didn't want to "retraumatize" a trans person—a thin attempt, mind you, to act like they really cared when in reality they wanted to exploit the "major transformation" that having a cis (usually male) actor playing a trans (usually woman) character would be dubbed—I thought her performance was what we needed at the time to move authentic casting conversations to the next stage.

Interviewing Isis for *Out* magazine, I asked about her time filming *When They See Us*. I wanted to know if she felt supported and affirmed throughout the process. She shared with me details about her audition for the role that touch my heart: "I got in the room, did the [post-transition character] and when I did the other one, I was like, 'I'm going to take my wig off,'" she said. "Ava was like, 'Are you sure? You don't have to.' I was like, 'I want to.' She was like, 'Okay, everyone turn around.' They were just so thoughtful about the situation and me being trans and being so respectful."

This care made me happy. Black trans women and femmes, and trans people at large, deserve care.

VIEWING GUIDE

AMERICA'S NEXT TOP MODEL (2003-2018)

Isis King competes on cycles 11 (2008) and 17 (2011).

AMERICA'S BEST DANCE CREW (2008-2012, 2015)

Leiomy and Vogue Evolution competed in season 4 (2009).

THE PRANCING ELITES PROJECT (2015)

Over two seasons, this Oxygen series followed the Mobile, Alabama, J-setting dance team that had gone viral on social media years prior. One of their members is a trans woman named Timberly Smith, whose depiction on reality TV did not conform to stereotypes.

STRUT (2016)

A show about trans models Laith Ashley, Dominique Jackson, Isis King, Ren Spriggs, and Arisce Wanzer that was an unprecedented look at the challenges they face navigating the fashion industry and everyday life.

HARSH REALITY: THE STORY OF MIRIAM RIVERA (2021)

A podcast hosted by actress and performer Trace Lysette that highlights the life of Mexican transgender model Miriam Rivera and her reality show *There's Something About Miriam*, which predated both Laverne Cox's and Calpernia Addams's reality TV stints.

WHEN THEY SEE US (2019)

Part four of this devastating, Ava DuVernay–directed series thoughtfully renders a trans character, pre- and post-transition, played by Isis King.

CHAPTER 4

LAVERNE

THE FIRST TIME I BORE WITNESS TO LAVERNE COX'S BRILLIANCE, I WAS IN GRAD SCHOOL AT STANFORD UNIVERSITY GETTING MY MASTER'S. It was the late spring of 2014, only ten months after *Orange Is the New Black* premiered on the then-new DVD subscription service turned streaming platform called Netflix. On the series about incarcerated women, which was based on Piper Kerman's 2010 memoir *Orange Is the New Black: My Year in a Women's Prison*, a forty-year-old Laverne played Sophia Burset, a trans inmate who committed credit card fraud to fund her transition since medical insurance would not cover it. I was a fan of the series, and especially of all the Black women whose characters that first season got the short end of the stick: Danielle Brooks's Taystee, Uzo Aduba's "Crazy Eyes," Samira Wiley's Poussey, and Adrienne C. Moore's Cindy, among others. So when it was announced that Laverne would be the keynote speaker of Stanford's Trans Awareness Week that year, I knew I had to be in the audience.

Laverne was on a speaking tour of sorts, giving her rousing "Ain't I a Woman? My Journey to Womanhood" talk. The title takes part of its name from Sojourner Truth's iconic

1851 "Ain't I a Woman?" speech, in which Truth argues the tenets of intersectionality, a word that would be coined by Kimberlé Crenshaw over a hundred years later, but in the context of rights for Black women, who were being left out of discourse as Black men and white women battled it out for who would get certain rights next.

"That man over there says that women need to be helped into carriages, and lifted over ditches, and to have the best place everywhere," Truth said during the Women's Rights Convention held at Old Stone Church in Akron, Ohio. "Nobody ever helps me into carriages, or over mud-puddles, or gives me any best place! And ain't I a woman? Look at me! Look at my arm! I have ploughed and planted, and gathered into barns, and no man could head me! And ain't I a woman? I could work as much and eat as much as a man—when I could get it—and bear the lash as well! And ain't I a woman? I have borne thirteen children, and seen most all sold off to slavery, and when I cried out with my mother's grief, none but Jesus heard me! And ain't I a woman?"

I was familiar with this speech, as it was one of the ones my South Carolina education emphasized during Black History Month. But to see it interpreted and employed by a Black trans woman, that was new. It was world-shattering to be exact, like taking the red pill and discovering that everything we've been told is a lie. That the gender I was nonconsensually assigned at birth in fact does not have to dictate how I move through the world on the daily. That life is already going to be hard, so why not live the fullness of one's truth in the process?

I don't remember much from the night, in terms of Laverne's actual words. But I do remember the goose bumps I got every time she would, after detailing the perspective of detractors who call her womanhood into question, fling her hair over her shoulder and say defiantly, "Ain't I a woman?" I remember the deafening applause of all the white folks who surrounded me in that audience. I also remember lollygagging around the outside of the building once the speech was over. I went to the speech by myself, so I had no reason to stick around, especially as crowds sometimes make me itch, and especially so when they're chock-full of well-meaning yet still annoying white queer people who will go up in the audience of Laverne's speech yet look right through me on campus. But I did hang around, fake-looking at my phone as many of us waited for Laverne to exit the building. To be honest, I felt a little like the woman in the Bible who just wanted to touch the hem of His garment, knowing she'd be healed. Or like the rabid fans who by hook or by crook end up in the arena pits of their favorite performer. For whatever the reason, I just needed to see her, offstage.

When she finally came out, flanked by campus security and event organizers, she was all smiles, simultaneously taking selfies with students and steadily making her way to a waiting car. I stayed back, choosing to avoid the stampede, just watching in amazement. Who would've thought that a Black transgender woman would be getting this type of response from all these white kids?

That night something unlocked in me. I don't quite know how to articulate what it was, but that "For Good" song from *Wicked* keeps playing in my head.

▬▬

2008 was, at one time, applauded as *that girl* for trans representation in media. In fact, by the year's end, *TransGriot*'s Monica Roberts dubbed it "The Year of the Black Transperson," noting "there were encouraging signs that the media blackout African-American transpeople have frustratingly endured and fought for decades may finally be starting to lift.

"Whether it was some African-American transwoman blogger whose commentary got posted on this blog, the Bilerico Project, and other various spots across the blogosphere to Isis King and Laverne Cox's star making turns on reality TV shows, 2008 will arguably go down as the year that Black transgender people got long overdue recognition and face time," she wrote.

A month before Isis's *ANTM* debut as a contestant, a pre–*Orange Is the New Black* Laverne Cox made history as the first openly trans woman of color to star on a reality show in the United States. A contestant on VH1's *I Want to Work for Diddy*, she competed against twelve others for the chance to become hip-hop mogul Sean "Diddy" Combs's assistant. Though she did not win, we must acknowledge how transgressive her casting was. To have a Black trans woman vying for such a position—in the world of hip-hop, no less—was, unfortunately, novel at the time because society had not often, if ever, seen a Black trans woman in white-collar spaces. "I think it's huge and it's so exciting for me to be a professional transgender person," Cox said at the time to *Black Voices*. "To see a transgender person on TV, hopefully people will continue to see us as human beings."

The series tied with *Transamerican Love Story* for the GLAAD Media Award a year later for Outstanding Reality Program. At the San Francisco ceremony, Laverne accepted the award, saying: "When you decide to be a contestant on a reality show, you sign your life away. And before I did that, I was clear and adamant with the producers and with VH1 that I did not want my representation on *I Want to Work for Diddy* to conform to the stereotypical and disparaging representations we've so often seen of transgender people and particularly transgender people of color."

2008, which Laverne has since called a pivotal year in her career, was also the year she booked one of her earliest professional roles, a drag queen named Candace who probably should've been written as a trans woman, on *Law and Order: Special Victims Unit*. The booking came after she had seen Candis Cayne on ABC's *Dirty Sexy Money* the year prior as Carmelita Rainer, a trans woman involved with Billy Baldwin's Patrick Darling IV. The role made Candis the first openly trans actress to have a recurring role in primetime. "It's just the truth that I wouldn't be here if it were not for her," Laverne told me in 2019. "That is the literal truth. I would not have believed it was possible."

Laverne's time on *I Want to Work for Diddy* opened up a number of doors, including one that led to the Mobile, AL, native becoming the first Black trans person to produce and star in her own TV show, 2010's *TRANSform Me* on VH1. The makeover series starred Laverne and two other trans women, photographer Nina Poon and makeup artist (who'd later star in the legendary series *Sense8*) Jamie Clayton. Together, they gave internal and external makeovers to cis women in need. The hope behind the show was to put trans people on TV screens inside the homes of middle America in hopes that people would see our shared humanity. But some trans people felt *TRANSform Me* reinforced stereotypes about trans women, Laverne told the outlet *them* in 2022.

In 2014, Laverne hosted and produced an hour-long documentary for MTV and Logo called *The T Word* that chronicled the lives of seven transgender youths ages twelve to twenty-four years old. When the film won a Creative Arts Emmy in the Outstanding Special Class category, Laverne became the first openly trans woman to win an Emmy as an executive producer, and *The T Word* became the first trans documentary to win an Emmy. But not before she found herself on the cover of *Time* magazine less than a year after *Orange Is the New Black* premiered.

It was late May/early June 2014. I was just days from embarking on a drive from Stanford in Palo Alto to El Paso, Texas, to drop off my belongings at my mom's house before boarding a plane to New York. The previous academic year had been a tough one for me personally. Having come into a secure-enough self while at Morehouse, I found Stanford a culture shock—and not just in the "I used to be surrounded by Black folks and now I can go two days and not see another Black person save the one Black woman in my program" way. I always say that I graduated Morehouse thinking I knew who I was, and that Stanford put that assertion to the test. But it was during that one-year program, all alone in a two-bedroom on-campus apartment I shared with another kid who barely spoke to me, that I bought my first pair of heels. I don't remember what brand they were or what they looked like, but I know they were from Payless!

As this shift was happening in my gender presentation, my resolve to tell the types of stories that most interested me—stories about Black and Brown folks, queer and trans folks in the community—to what felt like the chagrin of some of my professors, strengthened. It was clear to me that my program wanted to develop newspaper journalists, and I was not and did not want to be one of them.

But I did what I had to do, pushing back in class when professors would feature white journalistic accounts of Black trauma, challenging those in charge when my writing style would be questioned, calling into question the journalists and articles we were meant to revere and imitate. For whatever reason, my eye was always attuned to interrogation. This is important context because when Laverne's *Time* cover story, written by Katy Steinmetz, was released, I was literally in my last week of this program. Even more secure in the gender-full being I was becoming, I was with the shits, taking a critical eye at every article I read, especially if it featured Black LGBTQ folk.

To this day, I remember the feeling I felt reading the lede of the article: "In the beaux-arts lobby of the Nourse Theater in San Francisco, men in deep V-necks and necklaces walk by women with crew cuts and plaid shirts buttoned to the top," Steinmetz wrote. "Boys carrying pink backpacks kiss on the lips, while long-haired ladies whose sequined tank tops expose broad shoulders snap selfies. About 1,100 people, many gleefully defying gender stereotypes, eventually pack the auditorium to hear the story of an unlikely icon."

I was struck by the descriptors Katy used to paint a picture of the folks she saw. I tilted my head and squinted my eyes in confusion at what felt like and feels like a preoccupation with these people's bodies and how they adorned them, as if what she saw was odd or weird. Maybe it was, for her, but I sensed a perceived incongruence between how these people acted and the clothes they wore, and the bodies the writer assumed they were born into.

What follows is, today, an example of what not to do when reporting on trans people and gender-expansive communities. Carrying the headline "The Transgender Tipping Point," the article is an example of the toxic "both sides–ism" of journalism that platforms transphobes alongside us, delegitimizing our words and lived experiences. And she unnecessarily deadnames trans folks, like Christine Jorgensen and Janet Mock, as a, I don't know . . . manifestation of the "show, don't tell" style of journalism? Yet still, I was enraptured by Laverne's words, and her example. Of course, I had been a fan of her work on *Orange Is the New Black*, which had premiered the year earlier. While watching the show, I hadn't yet placed that I knew her from *I Want to Work for Diddy* years before. But to see her on that cover, in a simple blue dress, waist cinched . . . Her head is tilted ever so slightly high, an obvious sign of the confidence she wished to exude. But for me, it was the finger on her right hand. Someone would likely call the positioning of her hands graceful, like something an Alvin Ailey dancer might do at the beginning or end of a spellbinding performance—that special thing that shows an audience that the person they're looking at is as in control as possible. And Laverne did study dance at the Alabama School of Fine Arts; Indiana University Bloomington, on a dance scholarship, no less; and New York's Marymount Manhattan College, where she graduated with a Bachelor of Fine Arts in dance.

The finger, to me, was a sign of bad bitchery. The image did so many things for me that as soon as the issue hit news-stands, I bought a few copies. One of which I still have. It used to be framed in one of my old apartments, on a wall of personal inspiration that included *Ebony*'s February 1996 issue of the ladies of *Living Single*, *Out* magazine's May 2014 cover of Beyoncé, *Essence*'s May 2015 "Game Changers" cover featuring Debbie Allen, Shonda Rhimes, Issa Rae, Ava DuVernay, and Mara Brock Akil, and the final print issue of *Jet*.

"It's wild to me thinking about this magazine cover," Laverne told me in 2019. "Openly trans people on maga-zine covers [basically] did not exist before the *Time* cover." The only other instance she could recall of a trans person on a magazine in the moment, besides an *Essence* cover she shared with her fellow Black actresses from *OITNB* a year later, was Caroline "Tula" Cossey's 1991 *Playboy* pictorial. "It was really stressful, because . . . there's no amount of acting classes or life experience that can prepare you for that level of responsibility, pressure, and criticism, not just from right-wing people writing articles misgendering you, but also from your community itself," she said.

An unfortunate byproduct of the *Time* article was, in retrospect, an erasure of a history of trans people that had come before Laverne, in Hollywood and beyond. In addition to Candis Cayne, that included the likes of Alexandra Billings, Jazzmun Crayton, Sandra Caldwell, Ajita Wilson, Aleshia Brevard, and Candy Darling, among others. "We're on the shoulders of people who couldn't disclose, who couldn't be openly trans, who endured a lot worse," she continued. "I've always wanted to acknowledge that, that we know this isn't the beginning of all this."

Still, the importance of Laverne Cox's role on *Orange Is the New Black*, for which she became the first out trans actress to be nominated for an Emmy, cannot be overstated. A note: Angela Morley, a composer who died in 2009 at the age of 84, was an out trans woman first nominated for a Primetime Emmy for the score of 1983's CBS series *Emerald Point N.A.S.* And before that, Morley was the first out trans person nominated for an Oscar, for her score of *The Little Prince* in 1974!

Laverne's role unequivocally changed things in Hollywood. GLAAD's Nick Adams: "What I saw was that immediately after its premiere and people got to see the way Sophia Burset was written, and the way Laverne Cox was able to play her with such authenticity, depth, and humor—the overall conversation changed, [as well as] the types of requests that I was getting for consulting and help creating better transgender characters."

While we look back on the *Time* article today with a mixed bag of emotions, so much about who I am as a person and journalist I can trace back to it. Laverne's brilliance gave me greater resolve, and what I thought was a distasteful article made me want to help change how our industry reports on queer, trans, and otherwise fabulous communities. The article may have articulated what was seen as a trans tipping point in culture, but it was a personal tipping point for me, too. It was then that I started using the language of "gender nonconforming" to describe my unfolding gender expression and presentation. I started shopping, with greater regularity, in the women's section of the store, literally buying a whole new "professional" wardrobe for the fellowship program I was about to begin a week later in New York City at Logo and their editorial arm, *NewNowNext*. I had decided, in what felt like an instant, that if Laverne could be her most authentic self on the cover of *Time* magazine, I could do the same. Or at least try as I was still coming to trust my understanding of myself.

———

The first time I met Laverne Cox, I was a bundle of nerves. Not in that awkward, bumbling sort of way where I couldn't find words to speak. She don't do that. But in that "Wow, this person has really changed the game for a lot of people; don't fuck this up" type of way.

I was two years into my time at the *Los Angeles Times*. By this point, I had established myself through my reporting. The girls knew that Tre'vell was covering all things diversity. This became an asset for a number of the queer organizations in the city, finally able to get a journalist of my stature—their words, not mine, but honey they weren't lying!—to really see and engage with their events in the ways they hoped and deserved. That's how I got involved with Outfest, the Los Angeles LGBTQ+ film festival.

The summer of 2016, noted photographer Timothy

Greenfield-Sanders was releasing his HBO doc *The Trans List*, the latest installment in his "The List" portrait and film series. Inspired by a conversation with Nobel laureate Toni Morrison more than ten years prior, Greenfield-Sanders started photographing and interviewing notable African Americans for *The Black List*, a three-part documentary exploring Black identity. *The Black List*, which debuted in 2008, was followed by *The Latino List*, *The Out List,* and *The Women's List*. *The Trans List* featured interviews with a bevy of trans folks, from activist and Los Angeles legend Bamby Salcedo to icon Miss Major. Caitlyn Jenner was also in the doc, alongside actress Nicole Maines.

I believe it was Lucy Mukerjee-Brown, Outfest's then-director of programming, who reached out to me. *The Trans List* was going to screen at the festival, at the Director's Guild of America, and they wanted me to moderate the post-screening Q&A with Greenfield-Sanders, Salcedo, Angel, soldier Shane Ortega, and, yes, Laverne Motherfucking Cox. I jumped at the opportunity.

When the day came—according to the camera roll in my phone and Getty Images, it was July 16, 2016—I didn't know what to wear. My gender journey was still in flux, likely being read as an effeminate gay boy with a questionable sense of style. But, by this point, I had slowly come to perfect a base of a uniform of sorts for these types of events where I'd be on a stage. Its core was a pair of leather-ish leggings I got from H&M and my favorite black bootie heels that I purchased from Payless. Yes, this is the second time I've mentioned Payless. Before you continue judging me, let me say this: They were one of the few stores that I could go into that carried heels for what I call BFBs, big-footed bitches. I also hardly ever felt judged by the attendants as I jammed my bunions into a pair of Christian Siriano for Payless pumps. That welcoming environment—in the form of both the size availability *and* the lack of judgment—I realize now was pivotal for me. So, mind ya business!

But back to the leather-ish leggings and the booties. I had worn both of these items my first time meeting and interviewing André Leon Talley years later, but for Laverne, I paired them with a shapeless gray blouse of a moment that I knew wouldn't cling to my body, therefore the sweat that would invariably come to my underarms would just glide down the sides of my torso until it dried. And I hadn't yet found a barbershop environment in which I felt safe and actually listened to regarding my hair desires, so she was giving rough and rugged vibes in terms of the hair on my head and on my face. It was tragic, y'all. So, what does any auntie do when she needs to show out but her hair ain't did? I took a scarf that I rarely wore—I bought it while a student at Morehouse on a community service trip to Belize—and tried to do my best Jill Scott–Erykah Badu headwrap moment. It was Bad. Yes, with a capital B. But it's what I had, and I was confident in it.

Doing panels is weird, especially when you yourself are not also talent. These people didn't know me from Adam—yet—and so while the photos and whatnot were being taken before the panel, I awkwardly hung around, fake-reviewing my notes. I was introduced to all the panelists, and we were escorted into the theater and onstage. We did what we came to do. I doubt Laverne remembers this; I only remembered it in the course of writing this book. But I was so overjoyed at the opportunity to share space with her, especially after I had interviewed her over the phone a month earlier as the documentary she produced, *Free CeCe!*, about how CeCe McDonald, a Black trans woman, ended up in a *men's* prison and the campaign to get her out, premiered at the Los Angeles Film Festival.

The story goes that CeCe and a group of friends just wanted to make a midnight run to the store down the street from her Minneapolis home. But in the middle of their walk, a posse of white bar patrons accosted them. The instigators, men and women, lobbed a number of racist, homophobic, and transphobic slurs at the group before physically attacking them. McDonald eventually squared off with one of the male assailants, who, by the end of the altercation, died from his injuries after a pair of scissors pierced his chest, scissors that came out of McDonald's purse. This was the night of June 5, 2011, and McDonald was charged with two counts of second-degree murder. She pled guilty to second-degree manslaughter and was sentenced to forty-one months in, again, a *men's* prison. Unfortunately, this type of sentencing, in which trans people are incarcerated in facilities based on their sex assigned at birth, is not uncommon. A 2020 *NBC News* investigation by journalist Kate Sosin found that out of the 4,890 transgender state prisoners tracked in forty-five states and Washington, DC, the year prior, only fifteen cases in which a prisoner was housed according to their lived gender could be confirmed.

Free CeCe! follows McDonald for three years, connecting her story to the intersectional, systemic, and oppressive issues trans women, in particular, face, especially those of color. The doc features an interview between Laverne and McDonald in jail and McDonald's release after serving nineteen months, as well as her visits countrywide thanking supporters and advocating on behalf of trans people.

I was struck by this documentary largely because it came in a post–"transgender tipping point" era and at a time of then-unprecedented visibility of trans folks in media. Mind you, in addition to Laverne, *Transparent*, the Amazon Prime series based on Joey Soloway's own life in which one of their parents transitioned, had been drawing audiences and acclaim since a few months after the *Time* cover. Jeffrey Tambor, who is cis, played that transitioning parent, Maura, opposite a cast including Gaby Hoffmann, Amy Landecker, Jay Duplass, and Judith Light. The show was an instant critics' darling, nabbing Golden Globes and Emmys. It placed Tambor at the center of conversations about trans storytelling while highlighting the show's "transfirmative action" hiring philosophy that ensured trans people were employed at every level of production. Silas Howard benefited from this effort, becoming the first openly trans person to direct an episode of the show, a gig he told me singlehandedly changed the trajectory of his career. Having directed his first film, *By Hook or by Crook*, in 2001, he was working for and in community before *Transparent* gave him the access he needed to tell queer and trans stories on larger, less independent scales.

Caitlyn Jenner was also Caitlyn Jenner–ing, having shared her truth in front of the world in a *20/20* interview with legendary journalist Diane Sawyer in April 2015. She followed that up with an Annie Leibovitz–photographed cover of *Vanity Fair*, becoming the magazine's first openly trans cover woman, on which she declared, "Call me Caitlyn." There was also the E! docuseries *I Am Cait*, which followed her transition, its impact on the Kardashian-Jenner clan, and the former Olympian's growing visibility as a trans spokesperson nobody really asked for.

And yet, here was this film called *Free CeCe!* that was shining a spotlight on how visibility alone could never be our savior as a community. Because no matter what was happening on-screen and in pop culture, trans people were being jailed or even killed for defending themselves. Like Deshawnda "Ta-Ta" Sanchez, who in 2014, at twenty-one years old, was killed in South LA after being attacked, robbed, and shot. Or

Islan Nettles, who died at twenty-one years old in 2013 after a group of New York men battered her beyond recognition. Or Amanda Milan, who died at twenty-five years old from a knife attack to the neck by two New York men in 2000. In 2016, when the doc premiered, state legislatures were also already debating and passing anti-trans bathroom bills to restrict where we could pee.

This was the first time I began considering visibility to be the paradox that it is. I wasn't yet claiming the language of transness for myself, but I did recognize the ways my gender presentation could be interpreted and therefore put me in harm's way just for moving through the world as I desired and needed. I had already experienced such potential for danger just walking the streets of my South Los Angeles neighborhood nicknamed "the Jungle" for the lush landscaping early developers planted and not the reason most people remember it for, being a pivotal site in the 2001 movie *Training Day*. And that reality for many of us has only gotten worse as trans people continue to claim our rightful place in pop culture. 2021 was the deadliest year on record for trans people, with most victims being Black and Brown trans women and femmes. 2020 was the deadliest year on record before that, and 2019 before that.

——

The last cover I worked on for *Out* magazine as their director of culture and entertainment before being laid off two days before Christmas 2019 was the Culture issue that published in February/March 2020. I'd been in the role for a little over a year, part of the "Avengers of queer media," as the team editor-in-chief Phillip Picardi brought on was once called by *Out*'s then-CEO. Because the Culture issue was supposed to hyper-focus on Hollywood and entertainment, I was tasked with coming up with what our cover story and stars should be. I wanted to write a story that traced the industry's major changes in trans visibility since "the tipping point," from Laverne to someone like then-twenty-one-year-old gender-queer artist, model, and budding actor Chella Man. Both Laverne and Chella would be our cover stars.

It was arresting to witness the two meet for the first time on the day of our cover shoot, a sharp, early winter after-noon deep in Brooklyn. By this time, as I wrote in my *Out* story where some of this material was originally published, Laverne had been on set all morning dancing to Beyoncé and getting her Leontyne Price on, belting operatic riffs while in hair and makeup. As the set was prepped, Laverne was perched in her makeup chair like the titan of representation she is while Chella stood by her side sharing parts of his life story. We interrupted and escorted them to the photographer, hoping to capture this sharing of the torch of visibility. The pair cycled through a number of poses until Chella, almost instinctually, got to one knee. Gazing up to Laverne, he stretched his arms toward her, at once bowing to and reveling in her presence. "It's both corny and endearingly awkward, yet necessarily reverential," I wrote. "I can't help but think that it's exactly what he should be doing because, to put a spin on Martha Munizzi's popular gospel hit, he was created—as we all were—to make her praise glorious."

A week later, and the day before I got the formal notice that I, and almost the entire team at *Out,* was being laid off, I inter-viewed Laverne for the story at West Hollywood's Soho House. "Glorious" was exactly how she, then forty-seven years old, described meeting Chella. "I could cry. I really could . . . because I don't want to have children. But I kind of feel like these are my babies," she said of the new generation of trans people in

Hollywood, many more than half her age, for whom she was quite possibly the first trans person they saw on TV.

"Not that I've even met them or whatever, but it's like, this is the dream. This has been the dream for me," she continued, fighting back tears. "The only reason I did reality television is [because] I was consuming media years ago [and when] I watched *The Real World* and *Making the Band*, I was like, 'What would it be like if a trans person were on here?' Now we are, and it's just glorious."

First time meeting Laverne

VIEWING GUIDE

TRANSFORM ME (2010)

Laverne, Nina Poon, and Jamie Clayton give cis women makeovers in this VH1 reality series that ran for one season.

ORANGE IS THE NEW BLACK (2013)

The series ran for a total of seven seasons. Laverne was nominated in the outstanding guest actress category at the Emmys in 2014, when the show was listed as a comedy, and in 2017, 2019, and 2020, when the show was then considered a drama.

THE TRANS LIST (2016)

An HBO original, Janet Mock–produced extension of Timothy Greenfield-Sanders's List series that interviews notable trans people about their lives, including Caroline Cossey, Kylar Broadus, Amos Mac, and Laverne Cox.

FREE CECE! (2016)

This documentary about what was one of the most controversial imprisonments of a trans woman in America was produced by Laverne Cox as an extension of the narrative of her *Orange Is the New Black* character.

STAR (2016-2019)

While Laverne Cox is often credited in media as also being the first openly trans actress to be a series regular on primetime TV for her role in the 2017 one-season CBS series *Doubt*, that honor is actually Amiyah Scott's. Scott—who was an Instagram-famous model before becoming the first out trans person featured in the *Real Housewives* franchise on season 8 of the Atlanta version—starred in Lee Daniels's Fox series *Star*, which premiered before *Doubt*. Also starring Jude Demorest, Brittany O'Grady, and Ryan Destiny, the musical drama series follows three singers navigating the music industry.

"LAVERNE COX ON HER CAREER JOURNEY, FROM OITNB TO INVENTING ANNA" (2022)

In this YouTube video, Laverne traces her career for *them*, from dancing backup for the legendary Kevin Aviance to playing a cis woman in Shonda Rhimes's 2022 miniseries *Inventing Anna*.

CHAPTER
5

A TANGERINE GIRL

THEY DIDN'T WANT US TO SEE *GIRL*. The film was Belgium's
official submission for Oscars consideration that year, having won the most awards of any picture at the Cannes Film
Festival in 2018, and somebody thought that trans influ-
encers, critics, and journalists should not see a movie that
the broader cis industry was championing as great trans
storytelling.

   The debut feature of Lukas Dhont, who co-wrote it with
Angelo Tijssens, both of whom are cis, *Girl* follows Lara, a
fifteen-year-old trans girl, played by a cis actor, who dreams
of becoming a ballerina. With a supportive father by her side,
she grapples with the trials of attending a new school, training her late-to-dance feet, and living in a body she'd rather
not be in, all while starting hormone replacement therapy
and preparing for gender confirmation surgery. The film
was inspired by the real-life story of Nora Monsecour, who
at sixteen years old was the subject of an article in one of
the country's newspapers. The story goes that Dhont read
that article, contacted Monsecour, and got her permission
to make *Girl*.

The resulting picture gives "beautiful gowns" energy, to borrow a quote from the late icon Aretha Franklin. (When asked in an interview to give quick reactions to the so-called divas that had followed in the steps of Aretha's own divadom, in response to a prompt about Taylor Swift, she said, "Great gowns. Beautiful gowns.") Like, I can see why the picture won so many awards and garnered such acclaim from early audiences: the handheld-camera style characteristic of much of the contemporary European realism of the time; a seemingly powerful lead performance by a teenage boy who has to play a girl (and, hell, cis people love a fellow cis actor's transformation into a woman or girl, as seen in the cases of Jared Leto, Eddie Redmayne, and Jeffrey Tambor); and the presumed progressiveness of such a tale that highlights a sociopolitical environment drastically different than many of our real lives, as Lara is supported and affirmed throughout her journey in the film by her father and medical providers. But somebody didn't want trans people to see this movie, because they knew some shit was afoot.

In late October 2018, I was making preparations to leave my job as a film reporter at the *Los Angeles Times* to become *Out* magazine's director of culture and entertainment. In the four years I was at the *Times*, I created my own beat of diversity in Hollywood with a focus on Black and queer film, penning features that highlighted various inequities, including the lack of access for critics of diverse backgrounds and from smaller, less mainstream outlets. And because I was doing it at an outlet like *LAT*, the entire industry was consuming it. I note this to say that I had very little issues seeing the projects I wanted to see, in advance at private screening rooms or through viewing links. Color me surprised then when, after announcing I was leaving *LAT*, it felt like I was being run around when I inquired about getting a link or into a screening to see *Girl*.

Days earlier, I had received an off-the-record call from an advocate of trans storytelling in Hollywood who wanted to know if the film was on my radar. He then told me about the difficulty some other queer and trans critics seemed to be having getting access to see the film. Granted, it wasn't due to debut on Netflix until the top of the next year, which the platform was sure to note to *EW* weeks later when the magazine reported on the stark difference in opinion of queer and trans critics when compared to others. "*EW* was also told that critics largely haven't seen *Girl* because of the nature of this rollout. A special screening for LGBTQ tastemakers and Dhont is planned in the near future with additional press screenings in the works ahead of the film's release, which follow its run through the film festival circuit—including the LGBTQ-centric OUTshine in Miami."

But by that time, all of the award-season voting on nominations would likely have been done. If trans critics were going to have any chance to have our voices be part of the discourse on this film, we needed to be able to screen it like our counterparts. This contact told me about a screening that was being put on in a couple weeks as part of *Deadline*'s awards-contender series. He thought that that might be the best bet for us, considering the RSVP list was out of Netflix's hands and might not be monitored as closely. The date in question, and its location on the West Side, was not ideal for me. Still thinking I'd have the access that *LAT* afforded me, I promised to this contact that I'd see the film somehow and then make a decision about how to join the conversation.

After announcing my new job, I emailed Netflix and was put in contact with those handling *Girl*'s publicity. Upon clarifying that I'd be screening for coverage consideration at *Out*, not the *Los Angeles Times*, I reiterated a desire to get a screener link because my schedule wouldn't allow me to attend any of the FYC screenings I knew were happening. The publicist responded, imploring that watching it on my laptop or TV at home wasn't ideal: "The movie is so great-looking on a proper screen." Which is always an ironic response, I feel, coming from someone working for a streaming platform, but whatever. It was then that I decided to make the *Deadline* event work, shifting my schedule if need be.

When I arrived at the screening, which was set to feature a post-film Q&A with the director moderated by journalist Dino-Ray Ramos, I linked up with a couple queer and trans folks I recognized in line. Among them were journalist Zach Stafford, trans producer and media advocate Alex Schmider, and trans activist and author of *Sissy: A Coming-of-Gender Story* Jacob Tobia. After commiserating in line about how hard it had been to get to see this movie—some of us had to falsely RSVP for this screening as members of certain guilds and associations in order to gain access—we settled into our seats, all five of us sitting in one row, a few from the top.

As I wrote in my review for *Out*, "*Girl* is yet another example of what happens when the cis imagination gets ahold of trans stories." Its most offensive and violent part comes near its end. Heads up, I'm about to describe some graphic self-harm.

Throughout the film, it is clear how impatient Lara is for her body to finally match how she sees herself, even after her gender-affirming procedures are scheduled. So, to hurry her transition along, she mutilates herself. She calls an ambulance, attempts to numb her penis with ice, takes a pair of scissors, and cuts her penis off.

The scene is purposefully shocking, meant to demonstrate just how desperate Lara is to, using cringey language cis people often employ, "have her outside match her inside." Surely the creators behind it thought the scene would elicit sympathy and support for the experiences of trans people, and maybe it did. But the road to hell is paved with good intentions, and all I could think about was the message it might send to the little trans and gender-nonconforming kids who would stumble upon this film in their Netflix queue and do what kids do: follow suit.

"What's wrong with *Girl* is what's wrong with most projects that claim to represent the experiences of trans people with no substantive participation of trans voices," my review reads. "It's a missed opportunity to properly contextualize the experiences of trans folks coming into ourselves as more than purely physical and medical."

While I sat in the theater as the credits rolled, my row was silent as others applauded. Jacob, I believe, was the first to say something, making it clear that they planned to ask the director a question, if given the chance. We all pretty much agreed that what could've been a loving tale about a trans girl's coming into herself succumbed to the very stereotypes we all had been combating with regard to media representations. And it became clear to me why it had been so hard for many of us to get access to see it.

Mind you, this was in a post–Jared Leto in *Dallas Buyers Club* era, a post–Eddie Redmayne in *The Danish Girl* moment in time. Conversations about the importance of authentic casting had been had, in quite a mainstream way, too, following Scarlett Johansson's attempt to play Dante "Tex" Gill, a transmasculine person who operated a sex work and massage parlor in Pittsburgh in the '70s and '80s, in a film that was going to be titled *Rub and Tug*. And yet here was an industry going *up* for a film that not only cast a teen boy to play a trans girl, but one that used the excuse of being a film about dance to reproduce the shame and violence some trans people experience around our bodies for cis consumption; the camera unnecessarily lingers on parts of Lara's body, almost to the point of voyeurism. And the film does this without necessary interrogation of how those same cis audiences create and perpetuate the very shame and violence we as trans people sometimes experience.

As film critic Oliver Whitney would eventually write in a column for the *Hollywood Reporter*, *Girl* isn't "deeply humane" or "arrestingly empathetic," as non-trans critics described it. "It's sadistic exploitation made for uneducated cisgender audiences to *feel* like they get it. Dhont has done something far worse than make another clichéd and superficial portrait—he's disguised trans trauma porn as a triumphant survival story."

The film, while shortlisted for that year's foreign-language film Oscar, was not nominated.

━━

If Laverne Cox in *Orange Is the New Black* was supposed to be the "transgender tipping point," Kitana Kiki Rodriguez and Mya Taylor in 2015's *Tangerine* were the kindling meant to keep the fire burning bright. Or so we once hoped.

About a pair of trans sex workers who call a block of Santa Monica Boulevard their place of employment, *Tangerine* stars Kitana KiKi Rodriguez as Sin-Dee and Mya Taylor as Alexandra, two besties who've reunited on Christmas Eve after Sin-Dee finishes a twenty-eight-day stint in jail. When Alexandra accidentally reveals that Sin-Dee's pimp and boyfriend Chester has cheated on her while she's been away, Sin-Dee spends the rest of the day trying to find the girl he cheated with, Dinah, before confronting him. The film is a rollicking good time, dubbed by critics in the aftermath of its Sundance premiere a feat for both the acting performances and technical know-how. Famously, the movie was filmed on an iPhone 5s.

The *Hollywood Reporter* called it "a vibrant and uplifting snapshot." *Variety* reviewed it as "an exuberantly raw and up-close portrait." The *New York Times* said it was a "perfectly cast, beautifully directed movie," a "sometimes comic, sometimes melancholic journey into a little-seen world."

I was still a baby reporter at the time, and by "baby" I mean that I was less than a year into my fellowship with the *Los Angeles Times*. I wasn't yet using the language of transness to describe my lived experience. But I was very much gender nonconforming and Black as hell. The bio I wrote that introduced me to the newsroom months earlier said I was the love child of RuPaul, Wendy Williams, and Melissa Harris-Perry.

I can't remember the first time I saw *Tangerine,* but I do recall immediately buying into the hype of my colleagues and peers in the film reporting community. This was a time when I wasn't paying attention to the identities of those reviewing work on-screen, and how those identities might impact their receptions positively or negatively. Reading reviews that came out of Sundance, which often sets the stage for a film's trajectory—if it's panned out of major festivals like Sundance, its chances of catching on are tough; if it's praised, it's likely to have a longer shelf life that allows the film to pop up at the fall festivals and in conversations about awards season potential—it seemed like we had two new trans starlets to add to a still-too-finite list of trans talent that Hollywood can never seem to find. And with this "*Thelma and Louise*–style girlfriend comedy for our modern age," as one reviewer wrote, a messier, "realer" slice of trans humanity was welcomed. And in the aftermath of *Transparent*'s award-winning debut and Laverne's historic Emmy nomination for Outstanding Guest Actress in a Comedy Series in 2014, so many of us applauded what *Tangerine's* director, Sean Baker, was able to do.

By the time the film was released to the public that summer, Caitlyn Jenner had revealed her true self to the world, marking a high point for trans visibility on whose coattails *Tangerine* was able to ride. In October, *Variety* reported exclusively that Magnolia Pictures, the company that had bought *Tangerine* out of Sundance, and brothers Mark and Jay Duplass, who were executive producers, were launching an awards season campaign for its leads. It was the first time in history that a movie distributor had ever backed an Oscars campaign for trans actresses as they trumpeted Kitana in the best actress category and Mya for best supporting actress.

Even though neither of them landed an eventual Oscar nom, by November, they both were nominated in the Breakthrough Performer category at the Gotham Awards. Mya won, and was also nominated for best supporting actress for the Independent Spirit Awards. When she won that award, becoming the first trans actress to win a major film award after Harmony Santana was the first openly trans actress to be nominated for a major film award, in the same category, for Rashaad Ernesto Green's *Gun Hill Road* from 2011, Mya ended her speech making a plea for the industry to hire trans talent.

"There is transgender talent," she said, shouldering beautifully the expectations that had been foisted upon her. "There's very beautiful transgender talent. You better get out there and put it in your next movie."

During a recent rewatch of *Tangerine*, my first since that awards season ended, a different truth about the film was revealed to me. Sure, I still see how we all regarded this movie as the latest addition to the queer film canon, having rendered on-screen the lives of two Black trans sex workers with complexity in a way that may not have been done before on film. But *Tangerine* is also an almost ninety-minute accounting of a person's downward spiral of rejection. It hurt me to watch what is, as I see the movie in part now, a trans trauma tale wrapped up in a buddy-comedy bow. And this is not to say that stories about the challenges of survival sex work aren't worthy of being told, but *Tangerine* falls in a long line of narratives that reduces trans women, especially Black trans women, to the sex work they must engage in to survive—and though, yes, there are moments of levity and flickers of humanity afforded to Sin-Dee and Alexandra, they come only after the audience has seen both women experiencing varying levels of trauma, from the disappointment of being cheated on or ignored to being knowingly misgendered by cops and having a cup of pee thrown on them.

While watching, I also began to reminisce about the possibilities we all thought this film would bring for trans talent. To have an auteur, as the industry likes to call him, like Sean Baker put his cishet stamp of approval on trans actresses, and powerhouse producers the Duplass brothers affirm that choice by verbalizing a commitment to use their influence to get the film in front of the proper voting bodies—this was and is the type of allyship we talk so much about wanting and needing in this industry. But maybe we were wrong, or incomplete, in our thoughts. Because, with a little distance from that moment, we can see that it didn't actually shift as much as we'd hoped.

Tangerine and the discourse surrounding it is probably the first time I'd witnessed in the course of my gender and professional journey this form of what feels like the disposability of (Black) trans life. How they see and recognize our brilliance, and how, when they notice how it can bring them more recognition and fame, they exploit our rightful desire to ride the train till the wheels come off. But when it's all said and done, they move on to their next project and the apparatus that was created to try and get some awards attention is now gone. The flashing lights have dimmed. Red-carpet invites have slowed. And while there are auditions, and the roles appear to be better than they were, GLAAD's 2021 "Studio Responsibility Index," which surveyed the forty-four major studio films released in 2020, recorded nary a trans character. Not one trans character. In fact, there has not been a transgender character in a major studio film in three years as I write. "Factually, that is zero transgender characters across a total of almost 400 film releases tracked by this report since January 2017," the report reads. "The last transgender character GLAAD counted was an offensive caricature in the 2016 film *Zoolander 2*, a non-binary model named All portrayed by Benedict Cumberbatch."

The landscape of television, perhaps expectedly, is better—if we can even call it that. Of the 637 total regular and recurring LGBTQ characters counted on scripted primetime broadcast, cable, and streaming originals, 42, or just 6 percent, of them are transgender, according to GLAAD's "Where We Are on TV" report for 2021–2022. While an increase in the number of transgender characters compared to the previous year of the report, the stat also reflects a decrease in the percentage of transgender characters of total LGBTQ characters.

For all the progress we'd like to think we've made, we still don't have a trans movie star. Eva Reign did lead Billy Porter's 2022 directorial debut *Anything's Possible*, a coming-of-age rom-com centering a trans character. But being a *movie star* is different than starring in a movie.

This industry takes our stories, and weaves them into scripts they wouldn't have if our lived experiences didn't breathe life into them—with no formal writing or story credit!

Our "authenticity" elevates every line that is said, every shot that is filmed, every interview that is conducted. Promises of major opportunities to come swirl about amid handshakes from and acknowledgments by heavy hitters in the industry. We do the unthinkable and win a major film award and when it's all said and done, we're back to beating doors down, clamoring for people to see the talent. As writer Shaadi Devereaux notes in an essay titled "Beyond Representation" in volume 2 of the *Spectrum* insights report published in 2022 by Bold Culture, a data-driven, multicultural communications agency, "When you are visible, offers come to use that visibility in service of institutions, brands, and power, who seek narratives that do not ultimately challenge them but allow them to continue as usual, in exchange for letting a few of us in. After the door is closed again, the average trans woman is still in dire need of resources and societal protections."

Meanwhile, that auteur has continued to build his brand as the filmmaker who can turn poverty and trauma into Oscar bait with ease. But this isn't about him. Nor is it about, really, Mya or Kitana. This is about an industry that says one thing and does another, an industry that has always done this, but now trans folks are the latest casualty.

While watching *Tangerine*, a quote stood out to me. Walking down Santa Monica, Alexandra attempts to console Sin-Dee. "The world can be a cruel place," she says.

"Yes, it is cruel," Sin-Dee replies. "God gave me a penis. That's pretty cruel, don't you think?"

Indeed, sis.

———

There's a special predicament in which I find myself. I'm a Black, queer nonbinary person of trans experience who works in an industry that, in large, reproduces the very violence I navigate on a daily basis and challenge just by my very existence. We say we want to create an industry that reflects the fullness and vastness of our collective humanity, but when that stated goal might come in jeopardy—because the cultural productions that so much money has been spent to create about marginalized communities are often done without meaningful participation from folks in those communities, leading to said productions coming under fire—it quickly falls by the wayside. A small asterisk suddenly appears, leading to the fine print that says, "We only care about diversity, equity, and inclusion when it allows us to continue making money from our various cash cows. But cash is always king, so don't get too comfortable or too radical in your desires. This is, after all, a business."

That's basically what Netflix's CEO, Ted Sarandos, told the trans community, internally and externally, upon our outrage at Dave Chappelle's "comedy" special *The Closer* in 2021. When employees questioned how such a special with such trans-antagonistic and otherwise problematic assertions about the community could've made it to the platform—especially without any notice or consult of the trans employee resource group that had previously been consulted about other trans-related content—their boss gaslit them, and us. Sarandos told the world that the special would not be removed—which the group of employees who led this effort never asked for—because Dave Chappelle's content on the platform is highly engaged with. He all but said that transphobia was okay because they had paid Dave so much money in their deal and they needed to make sure they got their coins back.

Spotify's CEO, Daniel Ek, basically said the same thing in February 2022, when the streaming company came under fire for its refusal to manage the COVID-19 misinformation spread by its biggest podcaster and noted N-word user, Joe Rogan. "While I strongly condemn what Joe has said and I agree with his decision to remove past episodes from our platform, I realize some will want more. And I want to make one point very clear—I do not believe that silencing Joe is the answer," Ek wrote in a letter to his staff. "We should have clear lines around content and take action when they are crossed, but canceling voices is a slippery slope. Looking at the issue more broadly, it's critical thinking and open debate that powers real and necessary progress."

But he's only really saying all of this, to be clear, because they signed Rogan in 2020 to a multiyear contract worth more than $100 million. And though Ek would announce a commitment to invest $100 million in "the licensing, development, and marketing of music (artists and songwriters) and audio content from historically marginalized groups," all the historically marginalized groups wound up having to share a singular check, the amount of which they gave to Rogan alone. That's not equity. That's barely inclusion.

What then are those of us who live at the intersections of marginalized identities in this life to do when we're told by the men and women who pull the strings that affirming our humanity, or science, isn't worth it enough considering the other financial investments that have been made into people espousing hatred, confusion, and misinformation?

The Netflix/Dave Chappelle situation struck me as interesting as it unfolded, considering just a few years earlier I experienced what felt like an attempt to silence trans writers and critics about *Girl*—which itself was already perplexing considering Netflix's role in the "transgender tipping point" as the platform on which Laverne Cox was starring in *Orange Is the New Black*. With Dave Chappelle, it was the CEO who was leading the charge. With *Girl*, it was the people who oversee awards and publicity campaigns for the streamer. But the message was the same.

I constantly feel like my space in this industry, and the spaces of my fellow trans folks in most industries, is like that meme where the dog is sitting in a room that's on fire, sipping coffee, with a thought bubble that reads "This is fine." But it's not. Every day, something tries to kill us, to paraphrase poet Lucille Clifton. They try to kill our spirits, our imaginations, our desires for the land of milk and honey that we, too, were promised, and yes, sometimes they try to kill us. And every time we get back up, every time we find a way or make one, they fail.

But who wants to fight and agitate and push back and question and struggle in a burning house the rest of their life?

VIEWING GUIDE

TANGERINE (2015)

A sex worker tears through Hollywood on Christmas Eve in search of the pimp who broke her heart.

HER STORY (2016)

A web series of six ten-minute episodes, this show created by Jen Richards and Laura Zak follows the lives of two trans women (Richards and a pre-*Pose* Angelica Ross) and a queer woman (Zak) as they navigate the intersections of desire and identity.

UNA MUJER FANTÁSTICA (2017)

Winner of the Best Foreign Language Oscar in 2018, this Sebastián Lelio–directed drama stars Daniela Vega as the title character Marina, a waitress and nightclub singer who must put her life back together after her older boyfriend dies suddenly. But because she's a transgender woman, in a country with little to no support for trans people, she has to navigate cruelties lobbed her way both by her boyfriend's unaccepting family and the government. The film made Daniela Vega the first out transgender person in history to be a presenter at an Academy Awards ceremony.

CHAPTER
6

THE LAVENDER EXPANSES

I BEGAN MY JOURNEY TO NONBINARY BAD BITCHERY IN UNDERGRAD AT MOREHOUSE COLLEGE IN ATLANTA, AS I WROTE IN A PIECE FOR TORONTO'S *XTRA MAGAZINE*, WHERE I WAS EDITOR-AT-LARGE. Morehouse is the nation's only institution of higher learning dedicated to the education and affirmation of Black men. When I was a student, it was, initially, under the presidency of Robert Michael Franklin Jr., who created the Five Wells to govern the institution and how we, as "Men of Morehouse" aiming to become "Morehouse Men," should conduct ourselves. Under the Five Wells, we were to be Well Read, Well Dressed, Well Traveled, Well Spoken, and Well Balanced. The alma mater of the likes of Martin Luther King Jr., Julian Bond, Spike Lee, Maynard and Samuel Jackson, and Yours Truly, there is no place like Mother Morehouse. But I'm sure you can imagine what such a place—historically Baptist, a purveyor of W. E. B. Du Bois's "talented tenth" theory and super proud of the common saying "You can tell a Morehouse Man, but you can't tell him much"—might be like for queer and trans students on the campus. Your assumptions would be right for some of us, and wrong for others. Let's just say it was complex and *complicado*.

While I've always felt a slight dissonance between how the world referred to me and my internal truths, I chose the path of least resistance, settling as a gay Black man—until I couldn't any longer. My junior year, I stopped wearing suits; that was my way of breaking beyond what was expected of me. To do so at a place like Morehouse, where every freshman class is gifted a white button-down embroidered with our class year and a maroon blazer, and students dress in three-piece suits just because it's Tuesday, wasn't easy. It was during this time that I first began shopping in the "women's section" of stores.

As I prepared for grad school at Stanford, I waffled, outwardly and inwardly, in deciding on the language within which I found comfort. I always knew I wasn't a man or a woman as they're typically defined; I just didn't know what to call my gender. I started using "gender nonconforming" as a label to acknowledge my own growing understanding of self. I'd often say: "I exist not in the standard pink or blue, but in the lavender expanses of life." This approach helped placate the subtle and less subtle inquiries of family, colleagues, and peers, but it still didn't feel wholly right. But it was easier.

In 2016, I interviewed my Morehouse sister Fatima Jamal for the *Los Angeles Times* about her in-progress documentary *No Fats, No Femmes*. Throughout our conversation, she used "gender deviant" to describe her identity at the time. This rang in my ear like a cowbell at dinnertime. I remember having to fight with the *Times*' copy desk because such a declaration, paired with Fatima's pronouns at the time, which were "he-she," was new to them. Hell, it was new to me too, but I've long been a fan of the Maya Angelou quote "When someone tells you who they are, believe them." But it wasn't enough that Fatima had been intentional in the language she used to describe her lived experience to a journalist. This was somehow odd or weird, just because it unsettled and broke down the wo/man binary. I successfully lobbied to use both terms, an early win for me in my career.

The next year, Asia Kate Dillon burst onto the scene in Showtime's *Billions* as television's first major nonbinary character. I didn't watch the show, but seeing how Dillon navigated press as a nonbinary person was a window for me into the vast expansiveness of nonbinary experiences. But they didn't look like me, like, at all. Around the same time, I stumbled on the social-media pages of artist and performer ALOK, who is a must-follow on Instagram for their incisive and invaluable work to enlighten and degender the masses. In due time, I recognized that I was already familiar with ALOK's brilliance; they were a featured voice in Timothy Greenfield-Sanders's *The Trans List*, the HBO doc that led to my first time meeting Laverne.

ALOK also didn't look like me, in terms of their nonbinary experience. But they sure as hell were a lot closer. I became mesmerized by the ways ALOK would intersectionally dismantle all of the -isms and -phobias in a deeply coherent and passionate and poetic way. I felt a particular connection with them, having never met. I don't remember being able to articulate what was present for me through my cell phone and computer screens, but I knew I needed to keep my eyes tuned to them.

Shortly thereafter, I began mixing "nonbinary" with "gender nonconforming," becoming more able to better describe my gender as the pot of okra soup it is. Slowly, the other descriptors faded as I grew more comfortable in my nonbinaryness and a gender that is both specific and not, tangible and imaginative.

Still, when I think back on my journey, I'm forced to take stock of the host of words I tried on to describe my gender, and those I didn't, and the reasons why. One word that I avoided was "transgender." At the time, my understanding of the term was rooted in the very trans-essentialist, sensational, and dehumanizing preoccupation with medical interventions that the media and broader world force-fed me. I thought I couldn't be trans because I wasn't interested in engaging with the medical establishment.

And when I looked on-screen at the still-limited number of trans people I saw, no one who looked like me presented themselves like I was coming to present. I wasn't Laverne or Janet or Caitlyn. I wasn't Chaz or Zeke. I was all of them and none of them, but no one around me was really equipped to help me through those stages of self-discovery and identity. So, I made a home in "nonbinary," largely to myself, and just let others say and do what they please. Pronouns meant little to nothing. People could call me "he" or they could call me "she." And they could call me "they," though that was less likely. But as long as the name was spelled right on the check, I didn't care. Admittedly, in researching for this book, I've revisited many of the articles I've written over the years about trans-related things. In a commentary piece I wrote for the *Los Angeles Times* in July 2017, titled "Why it's time Hollywood let trans voices tell, and embody, their own stories," I do use the word "us" in talking about "trans and otherly gendered folk." It's unclear if I was naming myself as trans or otherly gendered or both.

Then, in 2018, I was contacted about participating in Sam Feder's documentary *Disclosure*, a then-unprecedented look at trans representation in film and television since the beginning of moving images. I was told about his personal mandate that every talking head seen on camera be a trans person, and how they thought I could add something to the conversation because of my reportage. I was also told that the bulk of the production crew was going to be trans as well, and that any person who wasn't trans on set was mentoring a trans person. I was impressed at the feat. Reminding me of *Transparent*'s "transfirmative action" policy, one that ensured trans folks were employed at every stage of production of the Joey Soloway–created series, this seemed like an approach to filmmaking with a similar intent. I knew I wanted to be part of it, but there was one question stopping me from immediately responding "Yes!"

Was I trans? I was a gender bender, for sure, just a-click-clacking my way onto red carpets and through the newsroom. More than just an effeminate gay man, definitely. But was I trans?

This was the first time I remember folks in trans community clocking my gender experience as a trans one. I was initially unsettled inside, intending to decline the invite to participate in the doc. But that outreach jump-started some very quick, internal work to unlearn everything I'd been taught about transness, and to divorce transness from the life-affirming surgeries and hormones some need.

I can't help but think about how my lack of knowing, my inability to see and claim what was obvious to others, was invariably connected to the historical medicalization of transness, a connection perpetuated by the narratives seen on screens large and small that wrongly assert a trans person *must* access hormones or gender-affirming surgeries. We have the cis imagination of transness, in the form of these transantagonistic storylines on TV, sensational segments on talk shows of yesteryear, and the legal landscape, to thank for this. The result was and is a tension between the overly simplistic social and cultural expectations often forced upon trans bodies and our lived experiences as those who desire and require medical transition and those who do not. And likely anyone embracing, consciously or otherwise, such cis-het presuppositions of transness reinforces the sociopolitical and emotional violence trans people face.

Because gender is a cell in which all people, cis, trans, and otherwise, are imprisoned by the prevailing binary beliefs about what it means to be a man or woman. It's a test every human being fails, consistently and gloriously; and yet our society is supremely invested in its maintenance. Being asked to be a voice in *Disclosure* was a catalyst for me to not only seriously process what my gender is and is not, but to find a community that could support that work.

═══

The first trans journalist I remember meeting is Monica Roberts. It was during my first National Association of Black Journalists convention, a joint one with the National Association of Hispanic Journalists in Washington, DC. This was 2016. It was in passing during a not-well-attended reception put on by NABJ's LGBTQ+ Task Force.

Monica always stood out in a crowd. Yes, because she was tall. But her infectious personality made her even taller and welcoming and warm. Her laugh, a signature one anyone who's ever heard it has come to love, showered any room in joy and ebullience. We met at the snackage, in a corner of the too-small reception room. I remember meatballs and cheese. She made a joke that I can't remember now. I chuckled; she laughed her laugh.

"I'm Monica."

"Tre'vell. Nice to meet you."

She went back to sit at the table where she'd been holding

court. I sat at another table; I was new to the organization, having attended "with" my *LAT* coworker and judy Brian De Los Santos, who was active in NAHJ. So many of the other queer people I had met throughout the convention at that point weren't at the reception. But Monica was.

Sometime later, before *Disclosure*, I stumbled on Monica's blog, *TransGriot*, which she founded in 2006. I can't remember how I found it, but I remember being taken by the idea that this Black trans woman had a blog dedicated to Black trans news and news Black trans people would care about. She had received a Special Recognition Award from GLAAD in 2016, and her acceptance speech was on YouTube. It was honestly then that I put the name and face together, that this was the woman I had spoken to over meatballs at NABJ.

TransGriot is an important archive of Black trans life. It is through the pages of Monica's site that I first learned of folks like Lucy Hicks Anderson, and Ajita Wilson, the Brooklyn-born trans actress who gained an international cult following in the '70s and '80s and was a *Jet* magazine Beauty of the Week in 1981. The public did not know Ajita was trans until after her 1987 death by brain hemorrhage following a car accident in Rome. And it was Monica Roberts, in the tradition of noted journalist and anti-lynching crusader Ida B. Wells, who best, and often first, documented the murders of trans people amid growing levels of anti-trans violence that the American Medical Association has since called an epidemic. As a one-woman news operation, she did what no other outlet—mainstream or otherwise—did: cover trans people and communities with dignity. Through her efforts, she recognized that cases involving trans victims hardly got solved largely because of the practice of police misgendering and deadnaming those killed. She also consistently called attention to and held accountable mainstream news outlets that, in following what police wrote in their reports, also disrespected trans people in their deaths. Her site became a clearinghouse of sorts, and a resource for mainstream news media in the pursuit of accurate, respectful reports. The intentionality with which Roberts reported was recognized by many in the community as necessary and vital work. "Monica wrote about things when no one else would, and she wrote about them with care," actress and advocate Angelica Ross told the *New York Times*. "She showed attention to the details, such as pronouns or naming us how we were known."

When I finally came into my transness, Monica's example kept me going. Anytime I questioned how a Black trans and nonbinary baddie like myself could do this work, Monica was who I thought of, and her tireless, industry-shifting work. If she could do it, I could too, I thought . . . I still think.

As cochair of NABJ's LGBTQ+ Task Force since 2017, I knew we had long wanted to recognize Monica for her contributions to our lives and the broader journalism ecosystem. It's why, in part, in 2019, we decided to make our annual convention reception in Miami into the LGBTQ Visibility Awards and Reception. We thought it would be a great opportunity to give Monica her flowers, but she, unfortunately, did not attend the convention that year. In response, we made an internal commitment to recognize her the next chance we got.

Monica Roberts died unexpectedly on October 5, 2020, at fifty-eight years old. Her sudden death sent shock waves through LGBTQ+ communities, leaving a craterlike hole in the media landscape where she once served as a possibility model for Black queer journalists and writers, especially those who are trans. Months later, I spearheaded an effort to create NABJ's Monica Roberts LGBTQ+ Task Force Scholarship as a means of honoring the legendary journalist and her commitment to the next generation of Black LGBTQ+ journalists and storytellers. I followed that up by nominating and successfully campaigning to have her included in the organization's storied Hall of Fame.

No accolade could really capture what Monica meant and means to so many of us, and I wish these honors from NABJ were bestowed upon her while she could still revel in the acknowledgment. But I do know she knew she was loved. We're all the better because she was.

━━

Disclosure: Trans Lives on Screen paved a way. Beyond what director Sam Feder, producer Amy Scholder, and executive producer Laverne Cox did in recognizing the me I was but wasn't particularly articulating, the documentary they created was and is pivotal for our ongoing discussions about visibility and representation of trans folks on-screen.

So many times in this industry, people feign ignorance about issues as it relates to diversity, equity, and inclusion because such concerns don't become concerns until someone provides a resource of sorts that says we should be concerned. That resource, unfortunately, must also be accompanied by enough outrage that those who stand to benefit from maintaining the status quo have to be compelled to pay attention and act. *Disclosure* did away with so many of the excuses.

"I knew from the beginning that it would only be trans people on camera and that I wanted to include as many trans people as possible behind the camera," Feder told me almost two years after I completed my interview for the doc, and just a couple weeks before the doc premiered at Sundance in January 2020. This was for a piece in *Xtra* magazine. "It was a no-brainer that if you're telling a history of a community, it should only be that community that tells it, as we are the experts of our own lives."

In just under two hours—and I'm sure Feder has many, many more hours of footage to fill two or three other docs— trans actors, creators, historians, and media professionals chart a comprehensive history of Hollywood's depiction of transgender people and the impact of those stories on trans lives and broader American culture. Upon being bought by Netflix, such a message, about the deleterious ways the industry has rendered our lives on-screen, became available to a worldwide audience. So much so that when someone, say, Netflix's own CEO Ted Sarandos, wrongly asserts that on-screen narratives *don't* lead to real-world harm, we can all point to *Disclosure* as proof that it indeed does.

The documentary has gone on to be a great educational resource for many. Oprah cited it as foundational prep for her interview with Elliot Page after the Oscar-nominated actor came out as trans and nonbinary at the end of 2020. Feder told *Vanity Fair* in 2021 that CBS's then-forthcoming show *Clarice*, which is based on *The Silence of the Lambs*, readjusted their production after watching the film, including hiring Jen Richards to both be in the writers' room and act on the show. "The series might have come out and perpetuated the harm that we see in *Disclosure*, but now that path is completely different," he said. Actor Ryan Reynolds also, apparently, reached out to Richards and Laverne Cox to say how the film impacted him, and he announced a fellowship he was developing inspired by the one *Disclosure* had with its production. Tracee Ellis Ross said on Instagram Live: "I didn't think this would resonate with me, but it completely aligns to how I was impacted by the media, and now I have a different language and framing for it, and I see everything differently now." Halle Berry was offered a role as a trans man in a film and she walked away not forty-eight hours after the *Disclosure* team asked her to watch their film.

And I'd be remiss if I didn't mention how participating in *Disclosure* gave me the permission I wasn't necessarily asking for at the time to write myself into the archive of trans visibility, to weave my story and lived experiences into that of transcestors known and unknown. I'm reminded of an interview Fatima Jamal did with Imara Jones for the TransLash Media short doc *The Future of Trans*.

"What is it that you're trying to create?" Imara asks.

"An archive," Fatima says quite simply, with a giggle.

"An archive of what?"

"An archive of my existence."

Disclosure cast

VIEWING GUIDE

THE FUTURE OF TRANS (2017)

Produced by journalist Imara Jones and her TransLash Media, the short doc explores trans futures with some of the brightest, sharpest, and most creative minds in trans and gender-nonconforming communities, including Chella Man, Patricio Manuel, Shea Diamond, and more. Available on YouTube.

RANDOM ACTS OF FLYNESS (2018)

The performance of gender is spotlighted on the second episode of Terence Nance's HBO late-night sketch comedy show. Through a series of monologues by a cis woman, trans woman, and gender-nonconforming person, gender is interrogated.

CALL HER GANDA (2018)

When twenty-six-year-old Filipina transgender woman and alleged sex worker Jennifer Laude is found dead with her head plunged into a motel room toilet, the perpetrator is quickly identified as nineteen-year-old US marine Joseph Scott Pemberton. The doc from director PJ Raval follows three people's efforts to investigate the case, including investigative journalist Meredith Talusan.

DISCLOSURE (2020)

An unprecedented look at transgender depictions in film and television, revealing how Hollywood simultaneously reflects and manufactures our deepest anxieties about gender, starring executive producer Laverne Cox, Lilly Wachowski, Yance Ford, Michaela Jaé Rodriguez, Chaz Bono, Yours Truly, and more.

CHAPTER 7

LIVE. WORK. POSE.

IT TOOK ME TEN MINUTES TO FALL IN LOVE WITH *POSE*, THE STEVEN CANALS–CREATED, RYAN MURPHY–BLESSED SERIES SET AGAINST THE BACKDROP OF NEW YORK'S UNDERGROUND BALLROOM SCENE OF THE LATE '80S AND '90S. The scene that got me was one just before the title sequence of the pilot episode.

Having resolved to walk the upcoming ball as "the Royal House of Abundance," Dominique Jackson's Elektra leads her children into a museum of fashion and design, where one of the displays is titled "The Royal Court." Upon an announcement over the intercom that the museum is closing, they scatter like roaches when the lights come on, hiding under and behind displays until the museum has been locked up. When the house emerges sometime later, they steal everything they can stuff into trash bags: petticoats and pantaloons, capes and collars, crowns and scepters. At the locked front door, Elektra quips, "I look too good not to be seen," before helping Jason A. Rodriguez's Lemar toss a nearby bench into the glass, triggering the alarm. The entire house runs in glee away from the museum, making their way to the night's location for the ball as cop cars tail them. When they arrive, they hastily put on their mopped garments as Billy Porter's Pray Tell starts commentating in the next room.

"Royalty. The category is . . . Bring It Like Royalty," he says, giving his best interpretation of the scene's commentators, as encapsulated in Jennie Livingston's landmark doc *Paris Is Burning*. (Livingston is credited as a consulting producer on *Pose*.) After a couple less-than-royal folks bring it to the floor, the House of Abundance makes its grand march.

"We're giving realness, we're giving capes, we're giving panniers and corsets and surcoats and crowns . . ." Pray Tell screams in jubilance. The house is soaking in the adoration of the crowd, and their tens, when the cops pull up outside. They bust through the doors, knocking over chairs in their way. Elektra sees they've come to get her and her children, but instead of putting up a fight, she quite gloriously offers her own hands to the police, a move that the crowd and I gagged at. The children of the house followed suit, shirking shame for pride at the stunt they'd pulled off.

"And that is how you do a ball," Pray Tell says.

Ten minutes, and I was hooked. This was a surprise to me, if I'm being honest. It's not that I didn't think the show would be good. Rather, there had been so much energy around the historic nature of the series that it felt like a letdown was in the cards. "These cis and white people are really going up for the trans folks on this show; it must be bad," I thought.

Months before I watched that first episode, all the entertainment websites could talk about, seemingly, was this new Ryan Murphy show that was going to push the discourse around trans representation forward, further than Laverne and *Orange Is the New Black* could and further than *Transparent* did. Initial announcements highlighted the fact that with the hiring of Michaela Jaé Rodriguez, Indya Moore,

Dominique Jackson, Hailie Sahar, and Angelica Ross, the show had the most transgender series regulars ever—and all Black and Brown—for a scripted television show. But there was also the historic hiring of Janet Mock, who became the first openly trans woman of color writer on a TV series, following in the footsteps of white trans women such as Our Lady J for *Transparent* (who was also in the *Pose* writer's room), Imogen Binnie for CBS's *Doubt*, and iconic trans siblings and *The Matrix* creators Lana and Lilly Wachowski for *Sense8*. Mock, at this point, was already a notable voice and presence in trans visibility. Following a 2011 *Marie Claire* article in which she came out publicly as a trans woman, the magazine editor published two books that became *New York Times* bestsellers, 2014's *Redefining Realness: My Path to Womanhood, Identity, Love & So Much More* and 2017's *Surpassing Certainty: What My Twenties Taught Me*. She hosted her own talk show, *So Popular!,* on MSNBC that "examine[d] cultural matters through a fun, cheeky, and thoughtful lens . . . and sometimes shady, too." Mock also produced *The Trans List* with Timothy Greenfield-Sanders.

In a column for *Variety*, Mock noted the ways that Murphy was taking a "back seat" with the series, being the good cis white ally by championing and centering the communities at the center of the narrative. "Not only is he donating all of his profits from *Pose* to organizations that directly serve trans and gender-nonconforming people (including the Audre Lorde Project, Fierce, House Lives Matter, and the Sylvia Rivera Law Project), he's empowered Canals and me, giving us unprecedented control of the narrative and direction of the show, urging us to cast nearly every part to ensure the show truly represents the characters on-screen," she wrote before the season one premiere. "We've casted and employed more than 100 trans people. This is extraordinary especially when trans people are an overwhelmingly underemployed demographic and have watched with gritted teeth as non-trans actors have embodied our realities onscreen."

This was all well and good, and worthy of all the celebration and attention it got. But the skeptical part of me couldn't fully indulge. My mind and eye kept focusing on other lines in the show description that most early reportage, in my opinion, seemed to deemphasize about the show. *Pose* was supposed to be a mid-'80s-set piece "examining the juxtaposition of several segments of life and society in Manhattan: the emergence of the luxury Trump-era universe, the ball culture world, and downtown social and literary scene," as *Variety* described the show back in 2017. It didn't premiere until 2018, and that Trump shit kept nagging me.

Mind you, Donald Trump was elected president at the end of 2016. He was sworn in on January 20, 2017, after full well showing his ass time and time again. We'd already heard him display his lack of respect for women with "Grab 'em by the pussy." We'd known already the outsized role he played in the trial against the now-renamed Exonerated Five, who were, as mere teens, wrongly accused of and imprisoned for the rape of a white woman in Central Park. We'd long known the absurdity of his antics, having consumed, quite joyously, *The Apprentice* and *The Celebrity Apprentice*. The idea that Trumpian foolishness was going to make its way into a narrative that was supposed to center Black and Brown trans femmes echoed in my ear like that annoying insect my granny always talked about sounding like it repeated "I know I know" over and over again. I needed to know what the hell that meant.

By the end of the first episode, I understood, as we're introduced to Evan Peters's Stan, who hires Angel (Moore) for a night of companionship. But Stan is married to Kate Mara's

Patty, who likes the new money her husband's Wall Street job is bringing in but not the man it's making him into. And there's Stan's boss, James Van Der Beek's grossly immature Matt. Both of them work under Trump in Trump Tower.

Every other scene of the show's first season features the unfolding narrative between this white, bougie part of society, and the lower-privileged of the ballroom scene. So, for all its history-making lore, we were gonna have to also watch some white and rich people drama. I couldn't help but think this was another example of the tired retort Black creators, and others of diverse background, often heard, though hopefully less so now, that they needed to write in white characters to give white people a way to see themselves in a narrative. Radha Blank's *The Forty-Year-Old Version* demonstrates this predicament with remarkable candor and comedy.

━━

I first caught a glimpse of Michaela Jaé's talent in the indie feature *Saturday Church*. From first-time writer-director Damon Cardasis, the 2018 film, which I saw during the 2017 Outfest Film Festival (mere months after Barry Jenkins and Tarell Alvin McCraney's *Moonlight* shattered an Oscars glass ceiling by winning, in an albeit chaotic manner, Best Picture), is the story of fourteen-year-old Ulysses, played by Luka Kain. A shy and effeminate kid grappling with questions about gender identity, their journey to self-discovery is invigorated after meeting a group of trans and gay folk who take the teen to "Saturday church," a program for LGBTQ youth held in the basement of a local church. There, Ulysses discovers a passion for, and family in, New York's ballroom scene.

Margot Bingham plays Ulysses's single mother. Regina Taylor is the devoutly conservative aunt. Rodriguez, Alexia

Saturday Church

Garcia, and Indya Moore, who would also be announced as a *Pose* lead months later, are members of the queer community, as is the legendary Kate Bornstein, the trans trailblazer, performance artist, and author of the seminal 1994 book *Gender Outlaw: On Men, Women, and the Rest of Us.*

Saturday Church came out at the height of early demands that trans roles be played by trans actors. While Jared Leto had won an Oscar for it in *Dallas Buyers Club* and Jeffrey Tambor had won two Emmys and a Golden Globe for it in *Transparent*, among numerous other cis people being awarded for playing trans characters, trans actors were coming together to say, "No more." They wanted to hold Hollywood accountable for its continued erasure of viable talent, and how casting cis people in trans roles reinforced "the notion that being transgender is a performance of sorts, that underneath whatever clothes trans people may be wearing, they are actually what their birth certificate says," I wrote in a 2017 column for the *Los Angeles Times*.

We were still at a point then when we needed to use a particular GLAAD statistic, that over 80 percent of people said they didn't personally know a trans person and that they got most (if not all) of their information about us via the film and television images that fill our screens, to convey the importance of authentic casting and the consequences of problematic trans narratives. Then there were the then-historic numbers of trans folks being killed, largely trans women of color. In 2016, at least twenty-two deaths were tracked by advocates, the highest ever recorded at the time. That number has risen every single year since, with 2021 ending with at least fifty-seven trans or gender-nonconforming people fatally shot or killed by other violent means. We say "at least" because too often these stories go unreported or misreported by police, medical officials, and the media.

Considering this, it was refreshing to learn the backstory of *Saturday Church*. Though writer-director Cardasis is not Black or Brown, nor a member of the trans or ballroom community, he was deeply influenced to write the film by a real LGBTQ outreach program at the West Village, New York, episcopal church St. Luke in the Fields. He learned of the program, called Art & Acceptance, through his Episcopal priest mother and volunteered with the group for a number of months during which he met members of the ballroom scene.

"Inspired by their narratives and their strength and creativity and their sense of empowerment when they performed," Cardasis told me for the *Los Angeles Times* upon the film's release, "[the film] took shape from there." But to ensure it felt authentic to the world he had volunteered in, especially as the film included song and dance numbers, he knew he had to cast people from that very program and the scene.

One of the ways Cardasis found his cast was by sending casting info directly to members in the scene, including dancer and choreographer Jose Xtravaganza, the father of the House of Xtravaganza, through Facebook. Through that posting, Garcia and Moore were cast. Garcia had always been interested in acting but had never auditioned for anything, and for Moore, their acting experience at the time was largely made up of training from the theater arts high school they attended. Other members of the House of Xtravaganza and members of the House of LaBeija were also consultants on the film.

Rodriguez was one of the most experienced trans actresses in the film, with acting credits including *Nurse Jackie*, *Luke Cage*, and an off-Broadway revival of *Rent* (she played Angel). She rounded out the cast and flexed some of those vocals we'd come to swoon over in *Pose*. But the entire film was yet another early example of how one might go about telling the stories of the ball scene and trans community when one isn't a member of it.

But there's a recurring quote that many trans actors were espousing at the time that ended up being co-opted and turned on its head. Moore said it to me in discussing *Saturday Church* and what set it apart from the likes of *Transparent, The Danish Girl,* and *Dallas Buyers Club.* "They don't have the emotional pull of what it's like to exist in that margin, what it's like to be unloved and rejected and the layers of trauma that come with being rejected so often by friends, family, [love] interests and for men to feel like it's okay to abuse you and have their way," she said. "[With us] it's not acting. We're actually pulling from an authentic place."

It is this sentiment—that of trans actors "not acting" when playing trans characters—that's been manipulated by other industry creators to the detriment, in my opinion, of trans opportunity in Hollywood and beyond. When trans folks say such a thing, it's meant to highlight the lived experience that an individual can use to undergird and reify their on-screen performances, to take something likely written by a cis person that lacks that special something that only someone who has lived the type of life written can unlock and make real. But for non-trans people, those directors, producers, casting agents, and more—when they say it, it's often to delegitimize and trivialize efforts to ensure authentic casting, to call into question attempts to hold them accountable for the perpetuation of tired tropes that continue to be spread when the cis imagination is the prevailing purveyor of trans imagery on-screen. It's also used to justify the way the industry persists in ignoring and refusing to recognize trans acting talent.

Let's talk about the awards ecosystem for film and television. By this point, we've debated the merits of awards shows like the Emmys and Oscars. Largely aided by #OscarsSoWhite, which creator April Reign and the broader community turned from just a social-media hashtag to an offline, industry-changing campaign, we've discussed at length the idea that we shouldn't put too much stock into awards bodies like the AMPAS, the Television Academy, or even the nominating committees for the NAACP Image Awards or the BET Awards. It's all a flawed system, as author and journalism legend Danyel Smith said on my podcast *FANTI* about the Grammys.

But it's what we have right now, she added, and the type of recognition that these bodies, especially the mainstream (read: white) ones, bestow on creatives can have benefits, career-wise, for those who find themselves among a group of nominees and especially those who go on to win. It's also important to note the difference in impact having, say, an Emmy or Oscar nomination or win for a white actor versus an actor of color. Throw in being queer or trans and the differences are starker. We absolutely should more readily engage in discourse about divesting from these entities, but that's a topic for another day.

Because at the same time, Michaela Jaé Rodriguez had the most overlooked performance of 2018. I wrote as much in an *Out* piece after noticing that the major awards shows seemed to only be recognizing the first season of *Pose* in one of two ways: the show either received a collective best drama series honor and/or Billy Porter was a best lead actor contender. There was so much hubbub around the show's historic nature—most trans series regulars ever on a single show; hired the first Black trans woman ever in a writers' room, etc.—but when it came down to the awards, the only person deemed worthy enough of solo recognition when compared to the broader landscape of category-appropriate performances was the cis guy . . . who, by the way, you—the entertainment industry—ignored and traumatized for decades? That felt off to me.

This was before Billy Porter would basically tell his trans castmates to mind their manners and wait their turn. "I've been in the business for 30 years. That's why I'm getting the attention. It just happens like that," he told *Essence*. "Patience, babies! I'm 50 years old. This is just happening for me." He sounded to me like the very white and more respectable gays back in the day that his character Pray Tell came to despise, though we know that wasn't his intention.

Billy very much was doing his good acting, of the high camp variety, and he deserved every honor that came to him. It *was* overdue. But the circumstances did strike me as . . . interesting, that the cis guy was getting acting nods, but none of his trans castmates were. After all, the Black and Brown trans women and femmes were supposed to be the center of the show. But I was particularly perplexed because Michaela Jaé's performance checked every awards-bait box.

I'd heard industry rumblings around the time that some anti-trans and/or ignorant fools believed Michaela Jaé and her castmates weren't actually acting at all. Employing the tired trope mentioned earlier, they said that she, as a trans woman, was not stretching herself in taking on this character. "But it is in this intimate knowing of Blanca that Rodriguez's skill shines," I wrote. "The truest, most pure part of the art of acting involves the task of becoming. The best actors don a persona and a being, allowing themselves to take a back seat in telling a most relevant story. They exhume the histories of our ancestors and allow them to inform their performance. They come to know the character, and themselves, beyond words on a page and offer onlookers the chance to get to know both at once as well.

"What Rodriguez has delivered, on every single episode of *Pose*, is the highest form of craftwork. She breathes life and struggle into the words of the script—which admittedly has its eye-rolling, ballroom 101 moments because cishets are watching. She capably shoulders a narrative that is sometimes campy, but always grounded and real. She rips her heart out, places it on the table in front of us and dares viewers to feel. And in exposing herself, she gives audiences the permission to do the same."

—

My chief hesitancy in celebrating what *Pose* was at the start was rooted in fear. In my short time in the industry, I'd seen up close how hope for a bountiful Hollywood career and the desire to keep an artistic flame burning could be snuffed out. How a show and its actors could fill a large hole in the television landscape, just for that hole to be left empty once the show was, as it always is, unceremoniously canceled. To me, it was great that all these Black trans people, and actual members of the ballroom scene, had jobs, and the types of jobs that might lead to increased sustainability for their art and livelihoods. But would they have careers? Was the industry really gonna shift, and in some meaningful ways, to rise to the occasion of the desires and needs of these Black and Brown trans folks? And if it did, would that *really* be the final crack in the glass ceiling of the moment? I knew many people were trying to make it so.

By the time *Pose* took its bow in 2021—after three seasons and twenty-six episodes—a believer was made out of me. Every single one of the trans leads had landed major roles or carved out new opportunities for their excellence outside of the show. *Pose*'s impact was undeniable, having caught the attention of the millions it entertained *and* educated.

Angelica Ross, whose fan-favorite character, Candy, was tragically killed off in season 2, landed a role in a second Ryan Murphy production, the FX anthology horror series *American Horror Story: 1984*. Such casting made her the first openly trans actress to secure two series-regular roles. And off-screen, she continued to be an advocate and activist, increasing the reach of TransTech Social Enterprises, a firm she founded in 2014 to help trans folks get jobs in tech. In 2019, she became the first openly trans person to host an American presidential forum, the 2020 Presidential Candidate Forum on LGBTQ Issues. Ross was also a producer on the web series *King Ester*, about a trans woman living in New Orleans as she navigates her identity and forges a path to stardom. The series was recognized at the Daytime Emmys with four nominations, including one for actress Rowin Amone.

Indya Moore, whose character, Angel, was based loosely off the lived experiences of pioneer Tracey "Africa" Norman—who at the height of her modeling career was outed as trans and subsequently blackballed until decades later—was featured in the Lena Waithe–written, Melina Matsoukas–directed 2019 film *Queen & Slim*. They're also in *Aquaman and the Lost Kingdom*, which as of this writing is slated for a 2023 release. Moore's growing career is perhaps most felt off-screen, though, having graced the covers of countless magazines and fronted fashion brands and lines. What's most remarkable, though, is how, for a period of time, Moore was one of the most visible nonbinary people, after asserting their identity in a since-deleted tweet: "I'm non binary, femme, Agender feels fitting too. My pronouns: they/them/theirs. I correct people often. At times they ignore me & I tolerate it to avoid conflict/irritation but it's upsetting to feel like I'm 'too much' in a world that takes so much from trans people constantly." This declaration forced many to begin using they/them pronouns in their speech, and journalists and news outlets in their articles, because of Moore's intense level of visibility. For a journalist who not too long ago had to fight to use gender-neutral pronouns for sources in articles, something like this mattered.

Hailie Sahar played Lulu, but never seemed to receive as much attention as her castmates. After *Pose*, though, she too went on to have other successes. In addition to landing roles on *Eastsiders* and *Good Trouble*, she cowrote, codirected, and executive produced *Beyond Ed Buck*, the 2022 documentary about the deaths of Black gay men at the hands of a wealthy older white gay man who was eventually convicted on nine felony charges for injecting some of them with fatal doses of methamphetamine. She's also teamed with noted director

Pose cast

and producer Anthony Hemingway for a biopic about trans icon Sir Lady Java, whom she will play. Sir Lady Java was a mainstay of the Los Angeles nightclub circuit back in the 1960s, sharing the stage with the likes of Sammy Davis Jr, Redd Foxx, Lena Horne, Richard Pryor, and James Brown until the LAPD decided to shut her down in 1967 with what was known as "Rule Number Nine," which banned "impersonation by means of costume or dress a person of the opposite sex." Sir Lady Java took the cops to court with the help of the ACLU. Though her challenge to the law was ultimately unsuccessful on a technicality—based on how the rule was written, only club owners (not performers) could sue—it paved the way for Rule Number Nine's eventual end two years later.

Dominique Jackson, whose reads as Mother Elektra are pop-culture iconography in their own right, had a three-episode arc on *American Gods*. Her modeling career skyrocketed, her aspirations toward which she first shared in the pre-*Pose* reality show *Strut*. Since *Pose*, she's walked in countless major fashion shows. She's also a hot commodity on the keynote/speaker circuit, giving powerful speeches about her journey at colleges and conventions nationwide.

And then there's the bleeding heart of *Pose*, Michaela Jaé Rodriguez. While the show was on the air, she starred in a Pasadena Playhouse reimagining of *Little Shop of Horrors* as its female lead, Audrey. I saw it, and really enjoyed her performance, a return to the stage where she got her start. She and her costar performed a song from the show on *The Late Late Show with James Corden*. And in addition to having a small role in Lin-Manuel Miranda's *tick, tick . . . BOOM!* in 2021, she released her debut single, "Something to Say." But perhaps the greatest sign of success came at the top of 2022, when she won the Golden Globe for Best Actress in a Drama Series, becoming the first out transgender actor to win a Golden Globe in the history of the awards. There was no formal ceremony, as we were all still navigating the coronavirus pandemic *and* the Hollywood Foreign Press Association was crafting its rebound after a 2021 *Los Angeles Times* investigation revealed its complete lack of Black members and other questionable operations.

But Rodriguez winning the Golden Globe was a huge moment for the community, after she had also made history the year prior by becoming the first-ever out trans woman nominated for a major acting role at the Emmys. But the singular moment that sticks out to me as most meaningful and representative of the impact of a show like *Pose* came in the form of the *Essence* Black Women in Hollywood Awards in 2020.

Essence, the legendary magazine created for Black women over fifty years ago, started its Black Women in Hollywood event back in 2007 to recognize Black women in an industry that often doesn't. Held during Oscars week, it's one of the most anticipated Black happenings of awards season, attended by everyone from Oprah Winfrey and Viola Davis to Janelle Monáe and Brittany Howard. The 2020 ceremony, a luncheon, honored *When They See Us* actress Niecy Nash, *Queen & Slim* director Melina Matsoukas, *No Time to Die* actress Lashana Lynch, and the cast and co-executive producer, director, and writer of *Pose*. It was, notably, the first time Black trans women had been recognized at the event in such a massive way.

As I wrote for *Xtra* that year, this is not to say that *Essence* had overlooked or ignored trans people prior, as the history-making brilliance of Laverne Cox and Janet Mock wouldn't allow for that. A year prior, the magazine's September issue featured a profile of trans actress Leyna Bloom written by Raquel Willis, for example. But for the industry titan and purveyor of Black womanhood that is

Essence to recognize five trans women and femmes in such a demonstrative way was moment-defining for me. In the audience, I found myself fighting back tears as they took the stage.

Flanked by an emotional Ross, Sahar, and Rodriguez—Moore and Jackson weren't in attendance—Mock, very aware of the cultural weight of the moment, said from the stage: "Too often, Black trans women and Black queer and gender nonconforming folk put their bodies on the line every day to be themselves, grappling with housing and joblessness and a lack of access to health care and education, and navigating our own people's intolerance and willful ignorance [that push] our sisters out of homes, intolerant schools, and churches, and into detention facilities, foster homes, prisons, and deeper into poverty. And these alarming issues remain widely unaddressed because we as a culture do not acknowledge that trans women are women, that Black bodies are valuable, and that Black trans girls and Black trans women are worthy of our protection and care."

She continued, saying, "The struggle for Black people must include Black trans and queer people. Period. And this award reaffirms that our stories, our lives, our experiences matter and reassures that the way that we tell it—from the perspective and talents of those who've lived it—is most impactful."

I still remember the moment her speech ended. The room rose to applaud. I could see others, folks who weren't trans or queer, also wiping tears from their eyes. I remember the chill that went through my body, because I had to latch on to myself to remain as present as possible in the moment, even as I was technically working. I hugged myself so tight, because I knew I'd just witnessed something glorious.

If *Pose* had done nothing else, it felt like in that moment, in that room, it had opened a door for Black trans women and femmes to not only continue to claim Black womanhood and femininity as our own too, but be welcomed into a Black sisterhood and femmehood we'd historically been excluded from. While Black communities are not innately more homophobic or transphobic than other communities, the reality is that countless queer and trans members of our biological families have been wiped out or otherwise marginalized by hate and ignorance. I knew, from experience, that Black queer and trans bodies weren't yet safe in many of our communities, let alone the broader world. That year, *Essence*'s Black Women in Hollywood luncheon made me *feel* the ongoing changes happening before our very eyes.

I ended my *Xtra* piece about the witnessing with a message to all of my Black trans siblings: "Keep living. Our mere existence, in all its God-given glory, changes the worlds we were born into. And when that shift manifests, you, too, will be in the room to witness it."

VIEWING GUIDE

PARIS IS BURNING (1990)

The canonical documentary from Jennie Livingston chronicles the mid- to late '80s era of New York City's underground ballroom culture.

KIKI (2016)

Cowritten by Twiggy Pucci Garçon and director Sara Jordenö, this doc picks up where *Paris Is Burning* left off, revisiting New York's ballroom scene and in particular, a subset of it known as the kiki scene.

POSE (2018-2021)

It gets even better after season 1, when the white cast members are removed from the story.

PIER KIDS (2019)

Written and directed by Elegance Bratton, the doc follows three Black, homeless queer and trans youth who call the Christopher Street Pier in NYC home. It was filmed over five years, 2011 to 2016.

DEFINING MOMENTS WITH OZY (2020)

Available on Hulu, the first episode spotlights *Pose* star Dominique Jackson's journey to celebrity.

CHAPTER
8

MASC FOR MASC

I DON'T THINK I EVER CONSIDERED TRANS MEN AND TRANSMASCULINE PEOPLE UNTIL I STARTED DATING ONE. To some of you, that sounds shitty and is likely something I should not be admitting publicly, let alone writing in a book. To others, you read that sentence like you read a menu at a restaurant, its contents barely registering. I'm inclined to agree with the former.

To admit that I didn't, haven't, or don't consider someone is shitty, and problematic. It's rude, erasive, and dehumanizing. Then to say I only began considering the lives of transmasculine folks when I found myself attracted to, desired by, and, eventually, in love with a trans man adds insult to injury. Now, situate that within a broader context of the ways trans men and transmasculine folks are particularly the objects of systemic violence, too. The sexual fetishization that reduces them to their bodies. The medical violence in the form of being denied health care procedures or suffering because of reproductive coercion. The disproportionate rates of incarceration that lead to 10 percent of trans men having spent time in jail or prison, a percentage that is approximately twice the rate of US adults overall according to the 2011 National

Transgender Discrimination Survey by the National Center for Transgender Equality and the National Gay and Lesbian Task Force. The experiences of victimization are rampant, further reproducing the harms I've already noted. My ignorance and unrecognition deeply troubles the more-aware me. The me who aims to be as expansive and as inclusive as possible in the ways I discuss trans visibility. Sure, the old adage "out of sight, out of mind" comes to mind here as an excuse or reason to write off such a revelation, and perhaps there's some truth to it. Yet upon deeper interrogation, I was part of the problem.

Ask yourself this: Have you ever *considered* transmasc folks? By "consider," I mean being inclusive of transmasculine, and otherly gendered, experiences in discussions of trans visibility that largely, and often only, center certain types of trans women. I'm talking about recognizing that liminal space under cisnormative and heteronormative patriarchy in which transmasc folks, too, are oppressed and marginalized, and being careful not to reproduce the same, or other, harms. By "consider," I mean not collapsing the worlds of trans men and transmasculine people into the very finite conceptions of manhood and masculinity that those of us in community are supposed to already be bucking up against and challenging.

The unfortunate reality is that many, if not most, of us haven't truly wrestled with such a question. We haven't confronted the ways our understandings and progressiveness can always be more expansive and more reflective of the multiplicities and complexities of the human and trans experience. And, in not doing so, our trans brethren and siblings and their desires and needs for, or dislike or rejection of, visible possibility models on-screen become an afterthought, a footnote, a whisper. Not often enough an organizing principle, a core bullet point, or a rallying cry in media. The visibility discourse in 2019 tells part of the story.

2019 was the twentieth anniversary of Kimberly Peirce's *Boys Don't Cry*, the film based on the real-life, tragic story of Brandon Teena, a twenty-one-year-old Nebraska trans man who was raped and murdered in 1993, that upon its debut was the first mainstream picture to focus on a transgender man. Hilary Swank won an Oscar for her role as Brandon. Chloë Sevigny, as the woman Brandon falls for, was Oscar nominated. That year, 2019, we'd also experienced another shift in the trans visibility conversation as trans men were cast in notable roles seemingly more often.

There was Isaiah Stannard on NBC's *Good Girls* and Alex Blue Davis on *Grey's Anatomy*. There was Asia Kate Dillon, who, after their 2017 *Billions* debut, starred in *John Wick: Chapter 3 – Parabellum*; and Logan Rozos in the Oprah Winfrey Network's *David Makes Man*, from the Oscar-winning playwright Tarell Alvin McCraney, whose unproduced play was the basis for *Moonlight*. There was Garcia, Marquise Vilsón, and others on Netflix's *Tales of the City* reboot. And that's just a sampling of transmasculine folks and characters from 2019 alone, and makes no mention of the trans men and transmasculine people who were taking up space in media with varying levels of regularity prior to, from Chaz Bono to Tiq Milan, Scott Turner Schofield to Kortney Ryan Ziegler.

2019 was also the year that Showtime's *The L Word: Generation Q* explicitly aimed to right the wrongs of its predecessor, which, back in 2006, introduced a universally despised trans character named Max. In case you weren't there, the original *The L Word* was *that girl* in a lot of ways. Having premiered in 2004, the show about a group of lesbian and bisexual friends upended prevailing depictions of queer women on TV. Whereas most queer women characters were window dressing for the heterosexual lead or some-how punished for their identities, *The L Word*, according to journalist Trish Bendix in the *Los Angeles Times,* "played a significant role in changing the perception of lesbians, offering a sexy, emotional melodrama to counter the absence of positive representation." When Max became television's first-ever trans man series regular character, the character played by trans nonbinary actor Daniel Sea was an "exciting development" for such a show made for and by queer folks. But Max's coming-out storyline was riddled with stereotypes and perpetuated trans antagonisms; he was ostracized by the women in his life and had violently angry bouts of mania after taking testosterone. The series ends with him dealing with an unplanned pregnancy and his future uncertain. Many trans men and transmasculine folks have complex feelings about Max. Because there was little to no other transmasculine representation at the time, many were and are grateful for Max's existence. But they're also frustrated, considering how the character came to represent for others the whole of a transmasculine person's experience coming into themselves.

With the reboot, the course was corrected in meaningful ways. In addition to the first season starring actors Leo Sheng and Brian Michael Smith as trans characters in sub-stantive, nuanced roles, author Thomas Page McBee was in the writers' room. Creative executive Tuck Dowrey was also assistant to showrunner Marja-Lewis Ryan, meaning a number of trans men and their perspectives were involved in the sauce that led to better, more reflective storylines. There shouldn't be narratives about trans men and transmasculine folks without trans men and transmasculine people behind the scenes, either.

But mind you, even as trans men and transmasc folks were

kicking down doors and carving out spaces for themselves in pop culture, so much of the popular discourse, which I participated in, focused on trans women and femmes. And while there had been prior moments of public discussion about trans men in media, 2019 seemed different. Notably, though earlier touchpoints focused on white transmasculine folks, we were now seeing Black, Asian, and Latinx trans men and transmasculine people as part of the conversation as well—five years after "the tipping point."

Since the start of my professional career reporting on LGBTQ+ film, I've always considered Kortney Ryan Ziegler's documentary *Still Black: A Portrait of Black Transmen* to be canonical. I had only ever really seen clips of the 2008 indie feature—I'm thinking a trailer, largely—until I started writing this book, but I knew that Ziegler's rumination on the experiences of Black trans men was a foundational text for contemporary conversations about the images of trans folks on-screen. I knew it was black-and-white and that it was a collection of six vignettes or mini films, each featuring a different Black trans man detailing his lived experience. I also knew it existed, and exists, as something singular and one of a kind.

An hour and eighteen minutes of Black trans men embodying the complexities of what it means to be—men who sometimes access masculinity and manhood differently than those who were reared as boys, more specifically—the film is a crash course in the expansiveness of Black trans men's experiences, and it is unfiltered through a cis imagination. It features Jay Welch, an Evanston, Illinois–based poet and musician; Ethan Thomas Young, a wheelchair user from Toledo, Ohio;

Carl Madgett, a Chicago-based church deacon and father of two; Louis Mitchell, a sober, LGBT diversity trainer with his wife in Springfield, Massachusetts; Nicholas Rashad, also in Chicago; and Kylar Broadus, an attorney who, four years later in 2012, became the first openly trans person to testify in front of the United States Senate when he spoke in support of the Employment Non-Discrimination Act.

Shot and edited over six months while Kortney was in grad school, *Still Black* came out at a time when Black trans narratives weren't the flavor of the month. Sure, Laverne Cox and Isis King were doing their things on reality television, but save talk shows like *Jerry Springer* or *Maury*, Black trans men and transmasculine people were hard to come by in media. And even now, as Kortney said during a University of California talk in the lead-up to *Still Black*'s tenth anniversary, "When people think of trans, in my opinion and from what I've seen, they don't necessarily think Black trans men. They don't really think that we exist actually, in so many ways."

Kortney surmises that this is because there is a fear in our society of Black masculinity. I'm inclined to agree, and the quantitative and qualitative data reflects this, especially when we look at how Black men, for example, are disproportionately targeted, stopped, searched, and killed by law enforcement. This fear, however, is not only white supremacist in nature but ultimately unfounded once we consider the ways our society has engendered us to look at Black men, and by ignorant association Black masculine folks, skeptically. This is not to say that Black men writ large haven't somewhat earned the bad rap they get; in an effort to navigate certain acts of violence, they've reproduced others on women and femmes, queer and trans folks, and themselves. Rather, it is to say that the project of imperialist white-supremacist cisheteropatriarchy is a heavyweight champion for a reason, and if we're constantly and only focused on the harm an individual *could* enact or perpetuate, we never really get to a place of attacking and eventually toppling the system that undergirds such potential behavior.

The result is that when we think of men and therefore masculinity, we automatically think toxicity and aggression and power and negativity. And when we think of women and therefore femininity, we think positivity and comfort and care and warmth. Such a binary leaves little to no room for those of us who find that our lived experiences necessarily complicate prevailing gender stereotypes. This means that broad strokes about men and masculinity never consider trans men and transmasculine people, and particularly how the truth and complexities of their existences might offer us as a culture other ways to see, hold, and grow alongside masc folks. In the same way trans women and femmes help further define and redefine womanhood and femme-ness, so can trans men and transmasc people help further define and redefine manhood and masc-ness.

And then when we specifically look at popular trans discourse, it is trans women and girls most often centered, and targeted. Many of the major visibility moments on-screen, especially those I've centered in this book, have been on the backs and labor of trans women. As I write, Republican-led state legislatures are introducing, debating, and passing laws that ban trans women and girls from playing on sports teams that align with their identities. The country is debating whether or not swimmer Lia Thomas, who in 2022 became the first openly trans athlete to land an NCAA Division I national championship after winning the women's 500-yard freestyle event, has an unfair advantage. And the vast majority of trans killings in the United States for the last few years have been of trans women and femmes, mostly Black ones.

Part of me believes that such a disparity in consideration of trans men and masc people and trans women and femmes is rooted in our culture's preoccupation with trans folks' bodies. Because of course, it's a lot easier to rouse ignorant folks when the conversation is about "men and their penises," which is what they call us femmes, trying to violate the sanctity of womanhood and their bathrooms and their sports. It's harder, it seems, to make the case that "women and their vaginas," which is what they might call transmasc folks, are similarly trying to infiltrate men's spaces. I think this is also where I'm supposed to say something about passability, or what's believed to be a greater ability for trans men, in particular, to blend in with cis society post-transition that evades some trans women. Because we all know and love short kings, regardless of their gender history. But for the tall glasses of water who are women, our society has always questioned their womanhood, and humanity—the dehumanization women like our Forever First Lady Michelle Obama and tennis superstar Serena Williams have faced, for example, is, in my eyes, eerily similar to that experienced by Laverne Cox or Angelica Ross.

So not only do many of us not think of trans men and transmasculine people when it comes to discourse about men, we also don't readily think of them when it comes to discourse about trans folks.

———

I've been racking my brain trying to remember the first trans man I saw in a meaningful way on-screen. Obviously, Chaz Bono comes to mind, but the awe and attention around his transition and subsequent visibility didn't ultimately capture my attention as a young whippersnapper. I also seem to recall a couple episodes of *Jerry Springer* that featured trans men in some sort of meant-to-be-salacious circumstance. But the one person that comes to mind most vividly is Laith Ashley.

It was 2016 and Oxygen, the cable network I'd fallen in love with a decade earlier when they aired *Mo'Nique's Fat Chance*—a pageant hosted by my favorite actress and comedienne of all time that featured ten big girls competing to become Miss F.A.T. (Fabulous And Thick)—broadcast a new show called *Strut*, about Slay, a modeling agency specifically for trans folks. I was there to watch Isis King; this was after I connected to her story on *America's Next Top Model* some eight years prior and I wanted to know what life was like for her now. Her cast mates included Arisce Wanzer, Ren Spriggs, a pre-*Pose* Dominique Jackson, and Laith—and y'all, he was, and *is*, foine!

Now the show only lasted for one season, but they packed a lot into each of the six forty-something-minute episodes. In addition to the professional woes everyone was navigating, audiences got a peek into the personal lives of the models. And while all of the ladies' journeys were of interest to me, it was Laith's—as a Dominican American man raised in a religious Harlem home—that stood out. As the only dude, his articulation of his experiences was naturally different than his other castmates', putting a spotlight on the specificity of a trans man's moving through the world.

A year later, in 2017, I saw headlines about Brian Michael Smith, an actor who'd been cast in the second season of Ava DuVernay's *Queen Sugar* and was using the role to publicly disclose that he was trans. I was already a fan of the Oprah Winfrey Network series, adapted from Natalie Baszile's novel of the same name, which follows the life of a trio of siblings in Louisiana after their father bequeaths them an 800-acre sugarcane farm following his death. Bicon Rutina Wesley, Dawn-Lyen Gardner, and Kofi Siriboe star in the hour-long drama alongside Omar Dorsey, Nicholas L. Ashe, Bianca Lawson, and the criminally underrated Tina Lifford. For the first season, I did an exclusive Q&A with DuVernay for the *LA Times* about a slowly unfolding storyline in which Blue, the son of Siriboe and Lawson's Ralph Angel and Darla, played by Ethan Hutchison, plays with a Barbie doll named Kenya. In my article, titled "A Black boy and a Barbie named Kenya: Why Ava DuVernay's *Queen Sugar* goes where many Black stories won't," I asked the *Selma* filmmaker about broaching what I read as childhood queerness in a decidedly Black and Southern story.

"I wanted to make sure that the story of *Queen Sugar* reflects all parts of our identity as Black people," she told me. "I want to start to interrogate the ways in which we embrace our identity, and that's happening with all the characters. Everyone is upside down with who they are and what it means to be someone else. It felt like there was a good opportunity with Blue to do the same, particularly around issues of identity as it relates to the ways in which we conform to certain notions of masculinity in the Black community."

"I'm really sensitive to the story line," she continued, "because I don't want it to be something that we're flag-waving or using as a big story point in a 'special episode of season 1.' I really want to start to seed it in. . . . This is a commitment from me and the writers to really explore this story line in a long-term way."

And that they did, crafting a beautiful narrative with Blue that unfolded throughout all seven seasons of the series. But the interrogation of Black masculinity happened elsewhere in the series, too, particularly with Brian Michael Smith's Toine Wilkins, a police officer and high school friend of Ralph

Angel's, first introduced in season 2. While the role is small, ultimately showing up in a total of three episodes over three seasons, Toine, who is trans, ends up being a catalyst for Ralph Angel to, eventually, do away with some of his toxic traits. In season 2, when Ralph Angel throws Blue's doll in the gas station trash behind his potentially queer child's back, it's Toine who reminds Ralph Angel that he protected Toine in high school from homophobic and transphobic bullies, and thanks him for it. "To have two Black men having this conversation about how to treat one another, expressing gratitude and being this open and vulnerable with each other . . . it was exactly everything that I was looking for," Brian said to me in 2019, reflecting on Toine years later.

In season 3, when Darla's mother calls Child Protective Services to try to get them to place Blue in Darla's sole care, it's Toine who calms Ralph Angel's nerves and reminds him that he's a good father. And in season 4, it's Toine who plants the seed in Ralph Angel's mind to establish a reentry program on his sugarcane farm for formerly incarcerated folks like Ralph Angel himself.

Watching the utility of this Black trans man—who, by the way, is never explicitly labeled as trans, though his gender journey is detailed in a thoughtful, caring manner—in such a narrative that champions Black Southern family and collective community, I could only smile each time Brian-as-Toine came on-screen. Because when I think of the types of narratives of trans folks I want to see more of, *Queen Sugar* is up there. So often, if TV and film is any indication, it's as if trans people aren't part of Black families and Black and Southern communities. And if we are, as you know by now, we're getting the shit beat out of us or are the butts of everybody's jokes. In *Queen Sugar*, though Toine is a tertiary character used to move the plot forward—like queer and trans characters typically are when we do show up on-screen—the character, in my eyes, is given more consequential responsibility than normal, and it was refreshing.

But what struck me more than what unfolds on-screen was Brian's choice to use the role as a vessel to come out as trans himself, after already acting on shows like *Girls*, *Blue Bloods*, and *Law and Order*—and playing cis characters, no less.

"This is definitely the time," Brian told Tiq Milan in a 2017 interview for *NBC*. After a few years of wanting to focus on the craft and taking roles that he was most comfortable with, a desire to bring his lived experiences into the work grew. "I was really trying to be cautious about it, because it was something I was interested in, but I wanted to make sure that it resonated with me, and it would have a positive impact on trans and non-trans people alike."

Brian credits Laverne Cox, GLAAD, and Tiq, among others, for helping to bring about such a moment where better-written roles for trans folks were created. And just a quick side note here: I don't remember the first time I came across Tiq and his work, but as Brian alludes to, he's another person whose visibility as an advocate, speaker, and writer was instrumental to the increase in representation of trans folks in culture, and Black trans men especially.

About working on *Queen Sugar*, Brian told Tiq: "Being able to work on a project like this that I believed in, that had strong storytelling and really interesting characters that are talking about real issues that are happening in the world and affecting our community, I loved that. This is the kind of work I've been interested in."

And the fact that this Black show from a Black network was the leading catalyst for Brian to make history upon his 2019 casting in Ryan Murphy's *9-1-1* spin-off, *Lone Star,* as the first out Black trans man in a series regular role—I have to stan.

━━

Well before Chella Man landed his first acting role, on the DC Universe superhero series *Titans,* the artist and writer had made a name for himself online, having created a community via a YouTube channel he started in May 2017. On it, he documented the process of, to borrow the title of the TEDx Talk he'd give a year later, "Becoming Him," educating what became hundreds of thousands of followers about what it means to be genderqueer, the effects of testosterone on his body, and gender dysphoria. By the top of the next year, Chella, who is Deaf, Chinese, and Jewish, also had a column called Man-Made with *them,* Condé Nast's LGBTQ+ outlet founded by Phillip Picardi; the column began seven days before Chella's top surgery. "I want to be the role model I never had as a kid," he wrote at the time. By September of that year, Chella signed as a model with IMG, an occasion deemed historic as he was the first Deaf, trans male model to sign with the international agency as the fashion industry was allegedly growing to be more inclusive. He subsequently was featured in campaigns for Calvin Klein, Gap, and American Eagle, among others.

Such a trajectory is a marvel when you find out that a few years earlier, Man was in the small, conservative town of Mechanicsburg, Pennsylvania, "trying to figure out how to live in a world where I had to lie about my true self, and simultaneously be happy and okay with that," he told me in 2019. "I was repressing my sexuality and gender, trying to figure out how to navigate growing up and educating myself in a space that wasn't designed for a Deaf person to learn in." And though he found bits and pieces of himself in pop culture—in the Freeform series *Switched at Birth* that ran from 2011 to 2017, model Nyle DiMarco, who won cycle 22 of *America's Next Top Model* (yes, they started letting men compete!), and sound artist Christine Sun Kim—freedom and acceptance seemed impossible at times.

By the time Chella had the opportunity to audition for *Titans*, however, he'd become vocal about the need for greater inclusion in media. So much so that just before he left the first audition for the show—which he credits his friend Lauren Ridloff, who starred on Broadway in *Children of a Lesser God*, for telling him about—he stressed the need for authentic casting, considering the role was for a mute character.

"I was like, 'If you don't cast me, you need to cast someone else who is disabled. You cannot give this to a hearing person,'" he told me. After leaving, he thought to himself that the casting directors "might be really annoyed that I was asserting my power, but that's the right thing to do."

Chella booked the role of Jericho, who, in the comics the series is based on, was rendered mute in an attack when he was younger and uses sign language to communicate with other members of the Titans team. The role debuted during the show's second season in 2019.

"My voice is now heard, and I'm able to be my own representation," he told me. "It's been a huge fucking privilege, and it's been absolutely amazing. I'm continuously learning so much about myself while being that person I wish that I had been when I was younger."

I spotlight Chella in this chapter for a number of reasons, but largely because, much like I felt when we decided that he should share the cover of our February/March 2020 Culture issue of *Out* alongside Laverne, his ability to be visible in the ways he's visible—and not just for trans and transmasculine communities—is proof of some sort of progress since "the tipping point." As is Elliot Fletcher, who has played trans roles on MTV's *Faking It*, Showtime's *Shameless*, and Freeform's

The Fosters; and Leo Sheng, who followed up *The L Word: Generation Q* with a role in the Lana Wachowski–directed *The Matrix Resurrections*, the 2021 sequel to the Matrix franchise, which we've all come to know is really a trans allegory.

The impact is made most clear to me in the words GLAAD's Nick Adams said to me in 2019: "For many years I've talked about the invisibility of transgender men in mainstream media and the implications that that has for young transgender boys who are growing up looking to see themselves somehow reflected in the media and see nothing, which makes them feel like there's really no place for them in the culture. So, while it's incredibly important that we continue to tell the stories of transgender women and transfeminine characters . . . it's also important that we tell more stories about transgender men and nonbinary people so that the full diversity of our community can be represented."

VIEWING GUIDE

THE BRANDON TEENA STORY (1998)

Beyond *Boys Don't Cry*, I recognize that many don't know the story of how Brandon Teena—along with Phillip DeVine and Lisa Lambert—was murdered. This documentary, directed by Susan Muska and Gréta Olafsdóttir, tells that story.

BY HOOK OR BY CROOK (2001)

Silas Howard cowrote, codirected, and starred in this queer buddy film about two unlikely friends, one of whom is a trans man, who commit petty crimes together, building a kinship in the process.

THE AGGRESSIVES (2005)

This pioneering documentary from Daniel Peddle was filmed in NYC from 1997 to 2004, following a group of "aggressives," or masculine-presenting and/or -identifying queer folks of color who were assigned female at birth.

STILL BLACK: A PORTRAIT OF BLACK TRANSMEN (2008)

Ziegler interviews six Black trans men about their stories of transition, their jobs and art, and how being a Black trans man engenders stigma for being trans *and* Black men.

BECOMING CHAZ (2011)

Directed by World of Wonder's Fenton Bailey and Randy Barbato, this doc follows the gender transition of Chaz Bono and includes interviews with his family.

QUEEN SUGAR (2016-2022)

Brian Michael Smith's character is featured in seasons 2, 3, and 4.

NO ORDINARY MAN (2020)

An in-depth look at the life of musician and trans culture icon Billy Tipton from directors Aisling Chin-Yee and Chase Joynt. Tipton was a jazz musician whose family and friends did not know he was trans until his death.

CHAPTER 9

BEYOND THE BINARY

I THOUGHT UNCLE CLIFFORD WAS THAT GIRL. After twenty-plus years largely struggling to see a character on-screen that looked and loved and sounded and lived like me, Nicco Annan's portrayal of the HBIC of the Pynk in the Starz series *P-Valley* felt familiar. Like that collard greens and cornbread Fantasia sings so fondly of. I've told you already about Darryl Stephens's Noah in *Noah's Arc* being an early site of possibility for me. There was also the late Nelsan Ellis's Lafayette in *True Blood*, which I discovered much later and still have yet to really study. But as I grew into myself, I felt Noah wasn't enough. Neither was the sometimes-unnamed sassy hairdresser on the periphery of *Girlfriends* or *Deliver Us from Eva*. But Uncle Clifford was different; it felt like, for the first time, a lived experience as complex as my reality was being rendered on-screen.

P-Valley, based on Katori Hall's stage play *Pussy Valley*, centers on a popular strip club called the Pynk in a fictional Mississippi town. Uncle Clifford, who uses she/her pronouns, is the Pynk's owner and mother hen who oversees a group of strippers. The hourlong stylized drama with plenty of comedy that Hall showruns herself intimately reveals the full lives of sex workers. Annan, who's gay, has lived with Uncle Clifford's character almost since its inception, having played her in the stage version.

The story goes that the two—Hall and Annan—came into each other's orbit through a mutual friend. When he got his hands on the script, Annan told me in a 2020 interview for *Xtra*, he was struck by the stage direction regarding Uncle Clifford, which read: "She emerges from the shadows, eyelashes like butterfly wings and nails like eagle talons. She is masculine and feminine in equal measure."

"I was like, 'What the hell is this? I'm here for it!'" he told me, finding the description of Uncle Clifford intriguing because it challenged the conventional approach he was taught to take as an actor who is also LGBTQ+. "I grew up under that pedagogy that in order to be good as an actor, you had to play straight." He described how professors made him feel like he would have less of a career if he couldn't "turn it off." But this character was a culmination of the synergy between Annan's personal and professional life.

I devoured the first season of the show, making it appointment television for myself every week as we delved deeper into the ways Black queer and gender-expansive folks move through our rural, Black communities—something we don't see much of on TV—in the form of Uncle Clifford. My heart fluttered as she developed a relationship with aspiring rapper Lil Murda, played by J. Alphonse Nicholson, even though he felt like he couldn't love or lust after her in public. Spoiler alert, honey: In the season finale of season 2, Lil Murda does love on Uncle Clifford in public. Yes, I was a puddle of tears. But back to my initial reactions to the series.

I found Annan's portrayal of Uncle Clifford to be fresh, and rooted in the truth of our humanity as nonbinary baddies who nevertheless persist despite all the -isms and -phobias that come up against us. And I felt like I could trust what was unfolding on-screen, because of the care Hall showed when talking of this character in interviews—Uncle Clifford is a composite of three people in her life: her mother, her father, and her real Uncle Clifford—and because the man who brought us *Noah's Arc* and whom I consider to be the father of modern Black gay cinema, Patrik-Ian Polk, was a co-executive producer.

About a year after *P-Valley*'s premiere, I pitched, produced, and hosted a podcast and companion video series with *Entertainment Weekly* called *Untold Stories: Beyond the Binary*. It was the second season of a limited series podcast *EW* had started the year prior during Pride Month. The first season was *Untold Stories: Pride Edition* to honor legendary LGBTQ+ entertainers in Hollywood history. That first season, I was brought in to narrate the pod, but for the second season, I wanted to take a more hands-on role. In recognition of the ongoing increase in nonbinary visibility, I wanted to speak only with nonbinary folks in and around Hollywood about the images on-screen that are said to reflect our experiences.

Mind you, this was just four years after Asia Kate Dillon on *Billions*, but so much had changed. Singer Sam Smith had come out as nonbinary in 2019; they detailed their journey to self for an *Out* magazine cover story that I helped book along with editor-in-chief Phillip Picardi. Elliot Page came out as trans and nonbinary at the end of 2020, becoming perhaps the most visible transmasculine person in culture at the time. When the podcast was released, UCLA's Williams Institute released a study of nonbinary LGBTQ adults that found that 1.2 million LGBTQ+ people identified as such, about 11 percent of all LGBTQ adults.

Here was the formal pod description:

Nonbinary people are experiencing a boom in visibility, from magazine covers featuring Elliot Page and Indya Moore to increasing numbers of nonbinary characters on screens large and small—not to mention the musicians and other creatives using their art to challenge gendered norms. Hosted by entertainment journalist Tre'vell Anderson, season two of EW's *Untold Stories* limited series podcast demystifies what it means to be nonbinary and analyzes the growing representation of the community via conversations with the nonbinary people paving their own paths. Together, they discuss the pop culture moments that informed their identity formations, the benefits and pitfalls of representation, and what the future of visibility looks like.

My producer was Carly Usdin, and they assembled an all-nonbinary team to help us execute the show in audio editor and mixer Samee Junio and video editor Aubree Bernier-Clarke. We interviewed fifteen nonbinary people for the series: actor Bex Taylor-Klaus from *Scream: The TV Series* and *Deputy*; writer and performance artist ALOK; comedian and drag performer Bob the Drag Queen; writer and model Devin-Norelle; author of *Sissy: A Coming-of-Gender Story* Jacob Tobia; actor Lachlan Watson from *Chilling Adventures of Sabrina*; musician Shamir; journalist and host of the podcast *Gender Reveal* Tuck Woodstock; creator of the animated television series *She-Ra and the Princesses of Power* ND Stevenson; comedian and actor River Butcher; actor Ser Anzoategui from *Vida*; musician Mykki Blanco; author of *How to Be You: Stop Trying to Be Someone Else and Start Living Your Life*, Jeffrey Marsh; creator of the Cartoon Network series *Steven Universe,* Rebecca Sugar; and singer Demi

Lovato, who came out as nonbinary in the middle of our production.

ALOK, the author of *Beyond the Gender Binary*, spoke about the importance of reframing our discourse as it relates to trans and nonbinary visibility, a concept that ultimately centers cis people because it regurgitates their ideas of what gender is, the idea that "we have to be some kind of spectacle that has to be visible when it's like, girl, we've been visible for thousands of years. You just weren't looking." The mere everyday existence, then, of nonbinary and trans folks is just as important as the images that make it to our TV and movie screens. And the type of content that *we* create that documents our mere existences—selfies on Instagram, makeup and styling tutorials on TikTok, sexy and raunchy flicks on OnlyFans and freak Twitters—is the vital creative act from which we should discuss our brilliance and genius.

"I really just love reframing the paradigm to be like, 'Nonbinary and gender-variant people are genius media makers and cultural workers because they made their life, and that's the ultimate act of culture in a world that has dispossessed them of history, of language, of family, of structure,'" ALOK said. "So rather than trying to get nonbinary and gender-variant people to manipulate our forms of media and existence into preexisting templates, meet us at our own templates."

This reminded me of something Nicco Annan told me in our conversation. When I asked about how he went about preparing for Uncle Clifford's television debut, he mentioned how he recognized that the stakes were different than with the stage production. "I did not want to get it right, I wanted to get it true," he told me. Nicco said he took inspiration from the source material and from Katori Hall's family members, the composite of which made Uncle Clifford on the page. And he thought about his uncle Bill, who was "sweet," as Black folks said back in the day, and wore a lot of bangles and bracelets. "You heard him when he was coming. You heard when he was leaving. You knew when he was upset because that wrist just got going."

Nicco also mentioned looking on social media and wanting to ensure his character wasn't lumped in with the history of cis, usually het, men donning wigs and makeup for comedic relief. He wanted Uncle Clifford to reflect "the truth to be told" of a nonbinary person's experience, which social media had given him a glimpse into.

So, when ALOK mentioned the creative genius trans and nonbinary folks were exhibiting on social media, it got me thinking about the ways in which those of us who are documenting our existences on these platforms become the research for those who don't live our experiences but are hired to embody them on-screen. The hashtags that we use so that we can locate and be located by our siblings in this jiggy jungle end up on the mood boards and the pitch decks of surely well-meaning individuals. But when there are benefits to be had—jobs, billboards, magazine covers, etc.—our essence is present, but our bodies are not. Our aesthetics make the cut, but we do not. Many other people, then, materially benefit from our special sauce as interpreted by someone else, and too often enough we never do.

I'm also thinking about the trans women whose names we don't know. The women who shared their lived experiences with Eddie Redmayne and Jared Leto to portray their roles as trans women. The women who helped Wesley Snipes, Patrick Swayze, and John Leguizamo into Noxeema, Vida, and Chi-Chi.

———

When it comes specifically to nonbinary representation, the people and characters in whom we most often see parts of ourselves reflected aren't necessarily nonbinary themselves. This goes for many people from communities often deemed marginal—Black and Brown people, disabled folks, non-Christians, etc.; we just sometimes have a tough time accessing images of true possibility. When we look at movies and TV shows and stage plays and the musical landscape, we're often looking at folks and characters meant to be stand-ins for all those who feel "different" or "eccentric" or "odd," as opposed to seeing lives and bodies and experiences reflective of our actual lives and bodies and experiences. That means we have to look at our pop culture images differently; we sometimes have to project upon and reinterpret what we see to affect some sort of belonging or affinity. Eat the meat, leave the bone.

We do this so much that our communities end up having our own canons of imagery of moments in pop culture that we recall as giving very much nonbinary tease, even though it actually isn't nonbinary. For me, I always go back to *The Powerpuff Girls*. Surely you remember Miss Blossom, Miss Buttercup, and Miss Bubbles, the girls made of sugar, spice, and everything nice with a heaping helping of Chemical X that turned them into superheroes. And you likely remember Mojo Jojo, the show's antagonist and top archenemy of the Girls. But my eyes were always glued to HIM.

I only recently learned that "HIM" is an acronym for His Infernal Majesty, but they were this flamboyantly fabulous villain from the animated series whose mannerisms were inspired by a character from the 1968 film *Yellow Submarine*, Chief Blue Meanie, according to series creator Craig McCracken. If you don't know who I'm talking about, imagine a red devilish figure with lobster-like claws and jet-black widow's-peaked hair. They had eyes the color of limes, each with only three eyelashes, a curled beard, soft rose cheeks, and a sickening black lip. And they wore this red jacket and miniskirt moment; it was unclear if it was two pieces or one, but there was also pink, cotton candy–like tulle at the collar and hemline, a black leather belt, and Lady Gaga–type black thigh-high spike-heeled boots.

I vividly remember something going off in my mind when I was younger that HIM was family! And not just queer, mind you. This character shape-shifted, and their voice ran the range of tone and sound; one moment it might be deep and hearty and what you might think of when you think of stereotypically masculine sounds, and the next it could be extremely light and soft and what comes to mind when you think of stereotypically feminine sounds. They had facial hair but loved some blush and mascara. Eyeliner on fleek, as the kids say. Oftentimes what we could see in terms of HIM's presentation of self, it gave very much gender abolitionist, and I was fascinated.

As part of the *EW* podcast, I asked all my guests about those moments in pop culture that felt nonbinary to them as they were coming into themselves. Here's some of what they said.

Lachlan Watson on *Silence of the Lambs*: "I got a tattoo because of how much I love *Silence of the Lambs*. It's a film that I recently, as a Gen Z trans person with a lot of privilege, look back on with a very different perspective from the trans people who grew up with that movie. When I watched *Silence of the Lambs* it felt extremely modern to me because Buffalo Bill, as a villain, never really self-identifies. Buffalo Bill never says, 'Well, I want to be a woman, so I'm going to kill people and make a woman suit.' Every single time Buffalo Bill is villainized or discriminated against, it is from the straight cisgender white guys in the FBI. They're the ones who decided, 'Oh, well, it must be because they're trans that they're killing people,' but that's not really the trans person's fault. I think this portrayal makes a better commentary on the societal reaction to Buffalo Bill as a person than it says about why Buffalo Bill was a villain in the first place, and I find that fascinating. We can (and should) be transgender *and* a villain, but only in a cisgender narrative do we become the villain *because* we're transgender."

Shamir on the Disney Channel Original Movie *Motocrossed*: "If you know, you know. If you don't, you don't. And if you don't know, I'm so sorry for you. I remember distinctly just being young and being like, 'She's killing it as a girl, she's killing it as a boy, and she's just killing it.' That movie made me nonbinary."

Jacob Tobia on *Sailor Moon*: "As a gender-expressive, gender-creative child, I remember being obsessed with *Sailor Moon*. I didn't understand my obsession as particularly queer or trans at the time, I just loved the show; especially the moments where Usagi (the main character) transformed from an average schoolgirl into Sailor Moon, a hero with powerful abilities and even more powerful accessories. Any show, especially animated shows that had 'transformation moments'—where a character went from their regular, day-to-day self to this opulent, incredible, powerful, rainbow-glittery version of themselves, the version of themself they must become in order to save the world—was a show that I loved as a kid. The subtext felt—and still feels—so trans, so nonbinary, so gender-transcendent. Shows like that really ingrained in me something of a mysticism around how I understood my gender and the power of femininity specifically."

Devin-Norelle on *SpongeBob SquarePants*: "I think we all read SpongeBob as a boy, but I always read SpongeBob as a fucking sponge that was whatever he wanted to be on whatever day. I never felt like SpongeBob had a gender. . . . There were days when he was trying to be the muscle bro. I love to be that person sometimes, but I don't want to be them all the time. Then he was playing with butterflies, and it's like, 'Wow, a masculinity that I can actually get with.'"

ALOK on Disney villains: "Because it used to be standard practice in this country to not allow any visible representation of queer people in media . . . oftentimes, the only representation of queer life we got was in Disney villains. People like Ursula, Cruella de Vil, these kinds of forms of femininity that were not necessarily linked to domesticity or being at home, or femininity linked to marriageability. I think so much of my nonbinary icons were these diva villains who I understood and had a deep resonant sense of being misunderstood and understanding that we live in a society where if you have a relationship with your femininity in that you own it and you're not apologizing for it, if you have a relationship with your femininity and it's not actually about trying to please men, people are going to demonize you. I didn't have the language to understand that, but I felt this deep resonance. When I think about my girl Cruella, it's like, the looks that she was serving, you knew she'd been through some tragedy. You knew that the only way that she could deliver the consistency of those looks was [because] she'd been struggling like me."

Jeffrey Marsh on *Wonder Woman*: "Lynda Carter's TV show, because she's going to the office, she's in a suit, she's in a pencil skirt, she's got her bag—'Somebody needs me? Let me just twirl around,' and here is all of this glam and fabulousness that also, by the way, can deflect the bullets of life coming at you, and can also force other people to tell the truth when you lasso them. The whole superhero vibe is very much to me a mirror of the transformation we go through to tell the truth about who we are."

=

Sort Of gives me hope. Created by Bilal Baig and Fab Filippo, the Canadian comedy series stars Baig as Sabi, a nonbinary millennial caught between multiple worlds: they're a nanny for an interracial family of two school-aged kids; a bartender at a local queer bar at night and on the weekends; and the youngest child in a Pakistani family in which being gender nonconforming is a huge social and cultural flaw. But as Sabi is experiencing the life shifts that come with balancing all they got going on, so too are the other characters in their orbit going through transitions of their own.

The story goes that this idea—that transition isn't just something that happens with trans people, as evolution is a quality of all humans—is what sold Baig on collaborating with Filippo. "Why should I, a Brown nonbinary millennial who feels like they might be transitioning, make a story about me with you?" they asked him, a cishet white man, before agreeing to collab. When Filippo responded that he, too, was going through a transition of his own—the ending of a fifteen-year marriage—and that he wanted to create a show where every character, not just the trans one, is in the midst of a transition, Baig was intrigued.

"There was a real power in acknowledging that it's a human experience to evolve, and the more we all embrace it, the better we all are," Baig told *Complex Canada*'s Marriska Fernandes. "It was with that, where we started to look at all the characters through that lens, like what is each of these characters' transitions? That really did it for me."

Such a positioning, they felt, aligned with their understanding of the impact they hoped their art can have. "I got very emotional because it also meant that if we can put work out into the mainstream like this, we really are at least evoking some conversations on what it means to evolve," they continued. "And I think what that does is it helps build empathy for trans and nonbinary people, because we're seen as the ones who evolve and transition in very particular ways. But when we can all tap into that for ourselves, I think trans and nonbinary people start to feel less like outsiders."

The result is an eight-episode first season that blew me away. Joyously mundane but not boring, the show centers Sabi in a narrative and a world where they could easily be on the periphery. And by treating the character as something other than the sassy, fashion-forward best-friend trope queer and gender nonconforming characters are often forced into, what seems so impossible for the broader media landscape is rendered possible. Quiet and intentional, but not hoity-toity or pretentious in its approach, it tackles the huge -isms and -phobias that nonbinary and trans people face in our everyday lives in everyday ways. Because sometimes the violence we face isn't as physical as the murders of Black and Brown trans folks and rather more subtle, like being offered support to find another nanny job by the father of the family that just fired you because of how difficult it might be, he says, "for someone like you."

Sort Of is different than anything else you've ever seen on TV, and not just because Baig is the first queer South Asian Muslim actor to lead a Canadian primetime television show. It's very familiar, having quietly carved itself a space alongside boundary-breaking, era-defining shows like Quinta Brunson's *Abbott Elementary*, Issa Rae's *Insecure*, Misha Green's *Lovecraft Country*, and Michaela Coel's *I May Destroy You*, among others. It's super specific but highly universal, in the same authentic, caring way a filmmaker like Barry Jenkins creates art about our lives as Black folks, from *Medicine for Melancholy* to *The Underground Railroad*.

When I now think about being seen on-screen, even as I rebuff the question, *Sort Of* is up there. It's still not my exact slice of life, and that's okay. But after feeling exhausted from being near the front lines of so much discourse about what our media landscape lacks, it finally feels like some of that possibility that we put into folks' imaginations about the validity of our stories is paying off. That those seeds we'd been sowing are sprouting.

We still gotta see what the harvest looks like, though.

VIEWING GUIDE

STEVEN UNIVERSE (2013-2020)

Created by Rebecca Sugar, the Cartoon Network animated series is applauded for how it addresses gender and sexuality in a way that youth and adults love and appreciate.

P-VALLEY (2020)

You've never seen a show like this on television.

UNTOLD STORIES: BEYOND THE BINARY (2021)

As a companion to the *Entertainment Weekly* podcast I hosted and produced, there's also a YouTube video series featuring interviews with all the guests.

SORT OF (2021)

It's a must-watch.

TRANSCESTORS

One of the byproducts of *We See Each Other* being a telling of a history of trans representation (largely) on-screen that is not chronological is that several trans folks and their contributions to the very moment we're living through—on camera and off—go unacknowledged, or underacknowledged. In this section, I wanted to highlight some of the transcestors whose bodies no longer roam this earth but whose gifts to (trans) culture opened a door or paved a path or otherwise made possibilities possible. I wish I could name them all. And yet, some of their names we may never know.

 **AJITA WILSON (1950-1987)** Born January 12, 1950, in Brooklyn, New York, Ajita was a model and actress. She began her career as a performer in New York's infamous red-light district in the early '70s. After being recruited into the porn industry, she gained a loyal following of fans as the star of numerous European softcore and hardcore adult films. Ajita starred in at least forty-six titles, a number that is surely not exhaustive. She was even featured as a *Jet* "Beauty of the Week" in the August 20, 1981, issue, the cover of which stars then-partners and actors Leon Isaac Kennedy and Jayne Kennedy (Overton). In the photo, Ajita is as free as the wind in a muted fuchsia two-piece, her hair in braids beaded in amber. Under the headline "Roman Beauty," the caption reads: "Beautiful Ajita Wilson from Rome, Italy, is a movie actress in Europe. When she is not making films, she enjoys reading, dancing

and people." Unfortunately, as Professor Matt Richardson notes in the 2020 *Transgender Studies Quarterly* article "Ajita Wilson: Blaxploitation, Sexploitation, and the Making of Black Womanhood," Ajita's film performances are the only accessible archive of her life. On the day she died of a brain hemorrhage, the result of a car accident, it was a sunny seventy-two degrees. That day was May 26, 1987. Only after her death did the world learn she was a woman of trans experience. When director Carlos Aured was asked to comment on what was then just speculation that she was trans, he reportedly replied, "She was charming, beautiful, and very professional. The rest is not important." I know that's right!

ALEXIS ARQUETTE (1969–2016) Alexis Arquette traversed

the gender spectrum throughout her forty-seven years of life. Part of the noted Hollywood family that also gave the world Oscar-winning actress Patricia Arquette, Alexis is perhaps best known for scene-stealing performances in 1989's *Last Exit to Brooklyn*, 1992's *Of Mice and Men*, 1994's *Pulp Fiction*, and 1998's *The Wedding Singer*. She documented her transition in the film *Alexis Arquette: She's My Brother*, which debuted at the 2007 Tribeca Film Festival, years before Chaz Bono's *Becoming Chaz* screened at the 2011 Sundance Film Festival. During Alexis's life, she was an art director for clubs, performed as drag queen Eva Destruction, and spent several years at Mattel as a toy designer. As she died, David Bowie's "Starman" played, part of instructions she left her family that also asked them to cheer "the moment that [s]he transitioned to another dimension."

BILLY TIPTON (1914-1989) Born four days after Christmas in 1941, Billy Tipton was a gifted jazz musician and bandleader. From the 1930s until the late '70s, he performed as a pianist and saxophonist throughout the country, from California to Idaho, Oregon to Missouri, where he grew up. According to the *New York Times*, an outlet that has and continues to perpetuate transphobia, Tipton was outed as trans on the morning of his death, January 21, 1989. The *Spokesman-Review* in Spokane, Washington, suggested at the time that Tipton began living as himself to improve his career prospects. His life story made national headlines, like "Musician's Death at 74 Reveals He Was a Woman." In 2020, the Chase Joynt and Aisling Chin-Yee–directed documentary *No Ordinary Man* premiered at the Toronto International Film Festival as an unrivaled portrait of Tipton's life that grapples with his complicated legacy. It was written by Chin-Yee and Amos Mac, who cofounded the legendary trans men's magazine *Original Plumbing* with Rocco Kayiatos.

CANDY DARLING (1944-1974) Despite living only to the age of twenty-nine, Candy Darling was a pioneering force in trans visibility in the late '60s and early '70s. Born November 24, 1944, in Queens, New York, to a bookkeeper mother and alcoholic father, she spent her childhood studying classic movies on TV and impersonating her favorite actresses. One of her favorite shows was *Million Dollar Movie*, a series that started in 1955 and ran for a decade that featured films like 1941's *Citizen Kane* and 1947's *Body and Soul*. Candy was one of Andy Warhol's superstar muses, alongside Holly Woodlawn (1946–2015) and Jackie Curtis (1947–1985). Andy cast her in his 1968 film *Flesh* after seeing her in a play called *Glamour, Glory and Gold* that also starred a young Robert De Niro. (Curtis, who wrote the play, was in it, too.) According to Warhol in his book *POPism: The Warhol '60s* (written with Pat Hackett), Candy wrote letters to the producers and studio that were making the 1970 film *Myra Breckinridge* asserting that she was the best person to play the starring role eventually given to Raquel Welch. After this disappointment, she went on to star in Warhol's *Women in Revolt* (1971)—as did Holly and Jackie—and other independent films, like 1970's *Brand X* and 1971's *Some of My Best Friends Are . . .* Candy was also once cast by Tennessee Williams—yes, *that* Tennessee Williams—in his 1972 play *Small Craft Warnings*. Before Candy died of lymphoma on March 21, 1974, she was immortalized in Lou Reed's 1972 track "Walk on the Wild Side." In 2005, Anohni and the Johnsons used Peter Hujar's photo of Candy on her deathbed as the cover of their album, *I Am a Bird Now*. In 2009, "the first transversal style magazine" was founded by Luis Venegas, titled simple *C☆NDY*, in honor, partially, of Candy Darling. Both Stephen Dorff and Willam Belli have portrayed Candy on film, in 1996's *I Shot Andy Warhol* and 2011's *Cinema Verite*, respectively. In 2019, it was announced that Stephanie Kornick was writing a biopic about Candy, executive produced by Zackary Drucker, a trans trailblazer in her own right, with actress Hari Nef (2018's *Assassination Nation* and *Mapplethorpe*) in the lead role.

JACKIE SHANE (1940-2019) Born in Jim Crow–era Nashville, Jackie Shane knew herself, and claimed as such, as early as thirteen years old. She grew up to become a force in Toronto's music scene as a soul and R&B singer, scoring the number two spot on the Canadian singles chart in 1963 with her cover of William Bell's "Any Other Way." Jackie helped shape the Toronto Sound, a style of R&B. It's said that after she relocated to Los Angeles in the early '70s, she turned down an offer to join George Clinton's Parliament-Funkadelic collective before retiring from music. She was barely thirty years old. Jackie lived largely out of the public spotlight until a CBC doc by Elaine Banks, titled *I Got Mine: The Story of Jackie Shane*, (re)introduced people to her in 2010. In 2017, the label Numero Group released a compilation album of Jackie's music, titled *Any Other Way*, with her permission. The album was nominated for a Grammy in the Best Historical Album category. In 2019, just weeks after giving an interview with Banks, Jackie died in her sleep at her home in Nashville. She was seventy-eight years old.

MARSHA P. JOHNSON (1945-1992) AND SYLVIA RIVERA (1951-2002) You should already know these two names, the close friends who founded the activist collective STAR in 1970. While Marsha's and Sylvia's places in the history of our collective liberation have recently been properly uplifted, I don't think we can ever give them their flowers enough. Marsha died at forty-five years old, just twenty-five days before my first birthday, on July 6, 1992.

Sylvia died five days after Valentine's Day, at fifty years old. The 2017 documentary *The Death and Life of Marsha P. Johnson* centers on activist Victoria Cruz's investigation into Marsha's death. The 2018 short film *Happy Birthday, Marsha!*, directed by Sasha Wortzel and Tourmaline, stars *Tangerine*'s Mya Taylor as Marsha, and actress and model Eve Lindley as Sylvia; it's an imagining of their hours right before the Stonewall Uprisings.

WILLMER "LITTLE AXE" BROADNAX (1916-1992) Willmer Broadnax was a gospel singer born in Houston, Texas, sixty years before Shirley Caesar became known as the First Lady of Gospel. His nickname, "Little Axe," came from his small stature, while his brother, William, who was a 5'7" baritone, was called "Big Axe." As writer Anthony Heilbut described in his 2012 book *The Fan Who Knew Too Much: Aretha Franklin, the Rise of the Soap Opera, Children of the Gospel Church, and Other Meditations*, Willmer's high tenor voice was "as sweet, clear, and poignant as that of his model, R. H. Harris. . . . Then, as quartet singers grew louder and blunter, he became a heroic screamer, holding his own with some of the strongest leads, Archie Brownlee or Silas Steele." Willmer worked with and was part of some of the biggest quartets in this era of gospel music, including the Spirit of Memphis, the Fairfield Four, and the Five Blind Boys of Mississippi. He also fronted his own groups: Little Axe and the Golden Echoes in the 1940s and Little Axe and the Golden Voices in the early '60s. It was not known that Willmer was trans, at least to the public, until his death on the first day of June, 1992. He was seventy-five years old.

AFTERWORD

I ALREADY TOLD YOU THIS BOOK IS NOT COMPREHEN-SIVE. And by now, you've realized that there are numerous instances of trans visibility on-screen since the beginning of moving images that I did not mention or reference.

Veneno, for example, the 2020 limited series about the life and death of Spanish singer and television personality Cristina Ortiz Rodríguez, better known by the nickname "La Veneno," could've been its own chapter. The Javier Ambrossi and Javier Calvo–created show, which after its airing in Spain was made available for streaming on HBO Max in the United States and Latin America, is a worthy example of trans storytelling done right, or at minimum a million times better and more complex and more reflective of the messiness of life that all humans know too well just with a trans lead. Invoking the concept of New Queer Cinema that critic and scholar B. Ruby Rich coined in 1992 to describe a break in LGBTQ+ filmmaking from heteronormativity and respectability, actress and model Hari Nef said of the series in *Artforum*, "If the New Trans Cinema is still to come, *Veneno* is an unprecedented example—on TV of all places!—of what it could be."

I could've also dived deep into *Her Story*, the Jen Richards and Laura Zak–created web series. Released online in 2016 as a collection of six ten-minute episodes, the show follows the lives of two trans women, played by Richards and a pre-*Pose* Angelica Ross, and a queer woman, played by Zak, as they navigate the intersections of desire and identity. "I had never seen relationships between trans women and cisgender women depicted," Richards told me for the *Los Angeles Times* then. "I had never seen friendship between two trans women—much less a Black woman and a white woman—or the issues of a trans woman who passes or issues with disclosure and what it's like to date." And so she made a show that reflected those things, one that was nominated for the Outstanding Short Form Comedy or Drama Series Emmy.

Or *Razor Tongue*, Rain Valdez's no-bullshit web series from 2019 about finding one's voice in a world filled with misogyny and discrimination that landed her an Emmy nomination for Outstanding Actress in a Short Form Comedy or Drama Series in 2020. The honor made her the second openly trans actress to ever be nominated for a Primetime Emmy in an acting category and the first Asian American—she's Filipina—transgender actress to be nominated.

I could've written a whole chapter about Scott Turner Schofield and the work he's done both in front of the camera and behind the scenes to help drag Hollywood to its current state. After making television history as the first out transgender actor in daytime television—he had a recurring role on CBS's *The Bold and the Beautiful* in 2015—Scott became the first out trans man to earn an Emmy nomination for acting, in 2020, for his recurring role on Amazon Prime's *Studio City*. Additionally, he consulted on HBO's *Euphoria*, helping to create what has been called "TV's most interesting trans character" in Hunter Schafer's Jules. He's also partnered with numerous organizations, including GLAAD, to educate thousands of crew members in on-set sensitivity. And he advised me when I first got into consulting!

I could've also waxed more poetic about *Jerry Springer* and *Maury*, and those infamous, salacious displays of trans life and beauty and mess that were both problematic for and aspirational to some of the trans folks who watched. Omissions like these, though, are just casualties of the form, and opportunities for the next trans and/or nonbinary writer to write themselves into the transcestry of their making and becoming.

In the course of writing, I've obviously been thinking a lot about visibility, more intently than normal. About it being a paradox, for sure, as Texas governor Greg Abbott tells his workers to investigate families with trans kids for child abuse simply for affirming their kid's identity, when one such parent of a trans child works in the very department that conducts said investigations. About our hard-fought gains, and the natural failures of visibility most often being about what does and doesn't appear on-screen.

In 2015, I interviewed Chaz Bono for the *Los Angeles Times.* He was starring in and producing a staging of Lee Blessing's *Down the Road* at Hollywood's Lounge Theatre. To be someone who blazed trails for trans and transmasculine people—not to mention the rest of the LGBTQ+ community—he seemed unfazed by the history-making laurels I was sure to mention. "I'm a guy just trying to make a living as an actor just like thousands of others," he said before adding, "People have a very fixed idea of me and who I am." He then described how that fixed idea, invariably the result of being an out, visible trans man years earlier—and the child of an icon—made it difficult for him to have the career he desired. It made it hard to get seen for roles and forced him, like so many other trans creatives, into producing just so he could work.

This is but one example of the not-so-positive byproducts of visibility that I'd like to see us talk about more, how blazing a trail can also create a limiting reality for both the trailblazer—and especially so for trans folks Black and Brown, femme and not, famous and less so, who don't come from the type of life that Chaz did—and those following the trail. Therein lies what Tourmaline, Eric A. Stanley, and Johanna Burton write in their introduction to *Trap Door: Trans Cultural Production and the Politics of Visibility* is "the trap of the visual: it offers—or, more accurately, it is frequently offered to us as—the primary path through which trans people might have access to livable lives." But said representation doesn't translate into bettered material realities for the trans folks not on our screens but in our neighborhoods. Visibility alone does not keep and has not kept the girls safe. It has not gotten nor does it get the boys trans-competent, affirming health care. It, alone, has not put nor does it put a roof over the heads of the enbys. Even as it helps some of us hold on a little longer, dream the impossible, and live out loud.

This is the part of the book and my journey writing it where I'm supposed to look to the future and pen a manifesto about the world I'd ultimately like to live in, the media ecosystem I'd like to see on screens large and small. But if I'm being honest, I'm tired of doing that.

I'm tired of naming and articulating futures that end up being masturbatory exercises for an industry not *really* invested in the type of unlearning and foundation-questioning necessary to get us to that Promised Land we all say we want. I'm tired of witnessing trans folks in this industry present ourselves as the antidote for so many of our industry's problems just to be gaslit and pigeonholed and told to be grateful things aren't as bad as they used to be. As Rain Valdez said in her acceptance speech of Outfest's Trailblazer Award in 2021, "navigating Hollywood as a transgender person can feel like a fruitless effort, despite the fact that we are the epitome of change in an antiquated system." I feel that deeply, even as someone who is not an actor or creator in the same ways.

"Forging a visionary path is really hard," she continued, speaking to the audience of the Outfest's Legacy Awards at the then-new Academy Museum in Los Angeles. "It's exhausting, lonely, and isolating. It can be physically debilitating, and it can lead you into a deep depression. Because you have to confront truths along the way. Like the fact that we know that visibility is no longer enough. And sometimes diversity is just pseudo-authenticity. And sometimes inclusion is just an invitation for us to witness the inner workings of our own oppression."

Yet here I am, still trying to do my part to push conversations along and support meaningful, transformative ideas that could upend the status quo as we know it. We're still here, like Tisha Campbell, evidence of the brilliance of what can be when trans imaginations come to life, and yet it feels like we're yelling into a void only to be heard by those who recognize the real in us, because it's in them, too.

In 2019, in recognition of the fiftieth anniversary of the 1969 Stonewall riots, the *Out* magazine staff came up with "fifty radical ideas for queer liberation." A package predicting, with jest and seriousness, the next half century of queer achievements, it was meant to be a jumping-off point for what our collective futures could look like. Things like a national day of service in honor of foremother Marsha P. Johnson. Or, on the one hundredth anniversary of Stonewall, then–House Speaker Alexandria Ocasio-Cortez immortalizing the event with the first queer dollar bill. I wrote number forty-four, the abolishing of gender-based awards show categories, and featured the efforts of Asia Kate Dillon on this matter. (By the way, in August 2022, Film Independent, a non proift that focuses on indie filmakers, announced its decision to join the Gotham Awards, British Independent Film Awards, Grammys, and the MTV Movie & TV Awards in degendering the acting categories for its Independent Spirit Awards, a conversation I and other nonbinary folks in entertainment were consulted about as early as 2020.) I also wrote number forty-five, about having Black trans folks leading a major Hollywood studio, managing mandates and controlling the coin purses.

"As Hollywood has begun to shift into an on-screen beast more diverse, inclusive, and representative of the sea of moviegoers—with writers, producers, directors, and other behind-the-scenes talent slowly following suit—studio executives with the power of the purse are still largely white, cis, and hetero men," I wrote then. "That means that for every Lena Waithe or Tanya Saracho or Justin Simien, there are five Bob Igers, a Jim Gianopulos, a Donna Langley, and all of their representatives from whom these queer creatives of color have to ultimately receive approval. So what might production slates look like if these studios were led by Black trans folk?"

I think of the stories, trans and otherwise, that they would have the opportunity to champion, the people who might get their big break because someone trans uttered "We see each other" to seal the deal as they chose to gamble on said up-and-coming or well-established talent.

It would be nice to, as the great songwriter once said, look back and wonder how *we* got over. To look at the transcestry of my making, alongside the transcestries that have made those who've come before me and will make those who come after, as continued proof of our community's brilliance.

ACKNOWLEDGMENTS

FIRST, GIVING HONOR TO GOD, WHO IS THE HEAD OF MY LIFE . . . I once said on a panel that God has to be a Black trans woman because it's Black trans women who most often show me what it means to be love embodied. I don't remember where I was in my gender journey at the time, if I had yet claimed my lived experience as a trans one. But thanks to all the girls nonetheless.

To my family, the one I was born into, I see your growth and I'm thankful for that. I love you like I love fried chicken and okra soup and macaroni and cheese. That's a whole lotta love, by the way.

To my sister Bianca Carter, a ride-or-die if and when I need one. We've been at this friendship thing for well over a decade, and you've witnessed the blossoming of the baddie I've become. Thank you for being in my corner and helping me grow.

To Mikelle Street, my South Carolina sister and one of the people I call when the dollars need to make sense and I need to be reminded of my bad bitchery. Your incessant, annoying check-ins were invaluable. Thank you for caring, and pushing me.

To Dr. Jared Loggins, a thought partner and confidant since our Morehouse days, and Dr. Higgins, an accomplice in the fight, thanks for your contributions to this here book, and my life.

To jarrett hill, my long-suffering collaborator from NABJ to *FANTI*, *Historically Black Phrases* to whatever the hell else we cook up together. You're welcome! And thank you for affirming my thinking when I needed it most. You also stressed me the fuck out. I know, we see each other!

To Texas Isaiah, you were there when I got the deal for this book. You helped open my eyes to many things. I'm happy about that, and grateful.

I have to give a shout-out to Patrice Caldwell, my agent, who heard my ideas for the types of books I wanted to write and said, "Let's do it." Then she waited patiently as long as it took me to put the idea on a page. I'm honored to be the client of such a badass Black woman. And thank you, Trinica Sampson, for keeping the train on the tracks!

Jennifer Levesque, my initial editor: Your enthusiasm never faded, throughout the many twists and turns. Aliya King Neil: It was your article, "The Mean Girls of Morehouse," that was pivotal in my development. To have you as the editor that helped me bring this book to the finish line is a full-circle moment I never imagined. Thank you both, and every person at Andscape that had something to do with getting this book out into the world.

Tuck Woodstock, your expertise made this book better. I'm grateful for your support. Amir Khadar, thank you for lending your artistic brilliance to the cover.

Nick Adams, the culture owes you so much. I'm honored to say that you've always looked out for me as you've looked out for the collective us. Thank you.

Lastly, to all of the people I neglected while trying to write this here book . . . y'all will be fine.

And remember to always slay on!

SELECTED SOURCES

Anderson, Tre'vell. "Isis King on Her Netflix Debut in Ava DuVernay's 'When They See Us'." *Out Magazine*, Pride Media, 31 May 2019, https://www.out.com/television/2019/5/31/isis-king-her-netflix-debut-ava-duvernays-when-they-see-us.

Anderson, Tre'vell. "'Next Top Model' Provided a Runway to Freedom for One Young Black Man Trapped by Gender Conformity." *Los Angeles Times*, 4 Dec. 2015, https://www.latimes.com/entertainment/tv/la-et-st-americas-next-top-model-20151205-story.html.

Anderson, Tre'vell. "What Does It Really Mean to Be Non-Binary? | Xtra Magazine." *Xtra Magazine*, 2 Feb. 2021, https://xtramagazine.com/culture/what-does-non-binary-mean-194517.

D., Trav S. *No Applause—Just Throw Money: The Book That Made Vaudeville Famous.* Faber & Faber, 2006.

Donnelly, Matt. "Ted Sarandos Doubles Down on Dave Chappelle Defense: 'Content Doesn't Directly Translate to Real-World Harm' (Exclusive)." *Variety*, 3 Oct. 2021, https://variety.com/2021/film/news/ted-sarandos-dave-chappelle-defense-1235088647/.

Feder, Sam, director. *Disclosure: Trans Lives on Screen.*

Feinberg, Leslie. *Transgender Warriors: Making History from Joan of Arc to Dennis Rodman.* Beacon Press, 2005.

Hernandez, Greg. "A Quick Chat with Calpernia Addams and Andrea James of 'Transamerica Love Story.'" *Out in Hollywood*, 29 July 2008, http://blogs.dailynews.com/outinhollywood/2008/07/29/my-chat-with-calpernia-and-and/.

Hilton, Perez. "The Bachelorette (That Used to Be a Bachelor)." *Perez Hilton*, 29 Nov. 2007, https://perezhilton.com/the-bachelorette-that-used-to-be-a-bachelor/.

Hinson, Mark. "Flying Home with The Lady Chablis Was a Blast." *Tallahassee Democrat*, 9 Sept. 2016, https://www.tallahassee.com/story/entertainment/columnists/hinson/2016/09/09/flying-home-lady-chablis-blast/90125768/.

Kacala, Alexander. "How Hollywood Heartthrobs and Steven Spielberg Helped Make a Drag Queen Cult Classic." TODAY.com, 3 Sept. 2020, https://www.today.com/popculture/how-steven-spielberg-made-film-wong-foo-cult-classic-t190808.

Kohn, Mitch. "The Amazing Story Behind 'To Wong Foo.'" *The Advocate*, 13 Aug. 2015, https://www.advocate.com/commentary/2015/08/13/op-ed-amazing-story-behind-wong-foo.

Marikar, Sheila. "Guy Turned Girl Seeks Love on Reality TV." *ABC News*, 30 Nov. 2007, https://abcnews.go.com/Entertainment/story?id=3933443&page=1.

Mock, Janet. "'Pose' Writer Janet Mock on Making History with Trans Storytelling (Guest Column)." *Variety*, 16 May 2018, https://variety.com/2018/tv/columns/pose-writer-janet-mock-ryan-murphy-column-1202803368/.

Parsons, Vic. "Trace Lysette wants the heartbreaking story of There's Something About Miriam to spark a reckoning." *PinkNews*, 31 Dec. 2021, https://www.pinknews.co.uk/2021/12/31/trace-lysette-something-about-miriam-harsh-reality/.

Roberts, Monica. *TransGriot*, 2006, https://transgriot.blogspot.com/.

Romano, Nick. "Trans Critics Explain the Problem with 'Girl' and Its Golden Globes Nomination." EW.com, 6 Dec. 2018, https://ew.com/golden-globes/2018/12/06/netflix-girl-backlash-trans-critics/.

Ross, Dalton. "Survivor Quarantine Questionnaire: Zeke Smith reflects on being outed as trans on the show." EW.com, 5 Mar. 2021, https://ew.com/tv/survivor-zeke-smith-millennials-vs-gen-x-game-changers-quarantine-questionnaire/.

Rustin, Emily. "Romance and Sensation in The 'Glitter' Cycle." *Australian Cinema in the 1990s*, edited by Ian Craven, Frank Cass, London, 2005.

Slide, Anthony. *The Encyclopedia of Vaudeville.* University Press of Mississippi, 2012.

Smith, Zeke. "'Survivor' Contestant Opens up about Being Outed as Transgender (Guest Column)." *Hollywood Reporter*, 20 Mar. 2018, https://www.hollywoodreporter.com/tv/tv-news/survivor-zeke-smith-outed-as-transgender-guest-column-991514/.

Snorton, C. Riley. *Black on Both Sides: A Racial History of Trans Identity.* University of Minnesota Press, 2017.

Stryker, Susan. *Transgender History: The Roots of Today's Revolution.* 2nd ed., Seal Press, 2017.

Townsend, Megan, and Raina Deerwater. GLAAD, Los Angeles, CA, 2021, p. 14, *Studio Responsibility Index 2021.*

Townsend, Megan, and Raina Deerwater. GLAAD, Los Angeles, CA, 2022, pp. 36–38, *Where We Are On TV 2021–2022.*

Whitney, Oliver. "Belgium's Foreign-Language Oscar Submission, 'Girl,' Is a Danger to the Transgender Community (Guest Column)." *The Hollywood Reporter*, 4 Dec. 2018, https://www.hollywoodreporter.com/movies/movie-news/belgiums-oscar-submission-girl-is-a-danger-transgender-community-1166505/.

Wigler, Josh. "Zeke Smith Speaks out About His 'Survivor' Experience (and That Very Public Outing)." *The Hollywood Reporter*, 4 May 2017, https://www.hollywoodreporter.com/tv/tv-news/survivor-zeke-smith-outed-as-transgender-voted-interview-1000082/.

FURTHER READING

Black on Both Sides: A Racial History of Trans Identity by C. Riley Snorton
This book directly confronts the erasure of Blackness in trans history by, among other things, surfacing the names and existences of Black trans folks in the mid-nineteenth century and beyond.

Trap Door: Trans Cultural Production and the Politics of Visibility edited by Tourmaline, Eric A. Stanley, and Johanna Burton
This anthology explores in great detail the many paradoxes, limitations, and impacts of trans representation. It features contributions from the likes of activists Miss Major and CeCe McDonald, director Sydney Freeland, and artist-writer Juliana Huxtable, among others.

Hiding My Candy: The Autobiography of the Grand Empress of Savannah by The Lady Chablis
I suggest listening to the audiobook, an abridged version of the physical text read by The Doll herself.

Spectrum, Volume 2: When the Image Speaks Back edited by Fatima Jamal
An insights report published in 2022 by Bold Culture, a data driven, multicultural communications agency, *Spectrum* is a vital offering on Black and Brown trans and non-binary folks' experiences in the media, marketing, advertising, and tech industries.

Belly of the Beast: The Politics of Anti-Fatness as Anti-Blackness by Da'Shaun L. Harrison
Exploring the intersections of Blackness, fatness, gender, and police violence, Da'Shaun challenges us to think more critically about the world we live in.

Mark 947: A Life Shaped by God, Gender and Force of Will by Calpernia Addams
It's important that we know the stories of trans folks who lived and loved before the "transgender tipping point." This is Calpernia's.

This Time for Me: A Memoir by Alexandra Billings
Born a few years before the Stonewall Riots, the veteran actress, whom I came to know via *Transparent*, recounts the evolution she's witnessed.

Dear Senthuran: A Black Spirit Memoir by Akwaeke Emezi
I profiled Akwaeke for a *Time* magazine cover. Their book changed me.

INDEX

A

Abbott Elementary, 206
ABC News, 95
Academy Awards, 9, 141
Adams, Nick, 10, 98, 115, 191
Addams, Calpernia, 2, 94–97
Aduba, Uzo, 107
Adventures of Priscilla, Queen of the Desert, The (film), 70–71, 84
Afro-American, 30
Aggressives, The (documentary), 192
"Ain't I a Woman? My Journey to Womanhood," 107–9
Akil, Mara Brock, 114
Alabama School of Fine Arts, 114
Alexander, Miss J, 61
Ali Forney Center, 88
Allen, Debbie, 114
allyship, 159. *See also* Murphy, Ryan
ALOK, 145, 198, 199–200, 204
Amblin Entertainment, 67
Ambrossi, Javier, 215
America's Best Dance Crew, 91–93, 105
America's Next Top Model (ANTM), 61–63, 87–91, 105, 185, 190
American Gods, 171
American Horror Story: 1984, 169
American Idol, 91
American Medical Association, 149
AMPAS, 166
Anang, Angele, 79
Anderson, David LeRoy, 52
Anderson, Lucy Hicks, 30, 149

Anderson, Tre'vell, 215–21
attending *When They See Us* screening, 102–4
creating trans representation timeline, 9–11
creating *Untold Stories*, 197–200
discussing Madea, 39–43
early life of, 7–8
escaping through film and TV, 8–9
in church, 21–25
interviewing, 116–21
learning trans history, 34–35
listening to Laverne Cox, 107–9
meeting Monica Roberts, 148–49
at Morehouse College, 14–15, 23–25
nonbinary bad bitchery of, 143–55
nonbinaryness of, 143–48
remembering Laverne Cox cover story, 112–16
reviewing *Girl*, 127–32
seeing Uncle Clifford on-screen, 195–97
on seeing themself, 59–63
seeing Isis King, 87–91
seeing Leiomy Maldonado, 91–93
watching *Boys Don't Cry*, 11–12
watching *Pose*, 157–61
working on *Out* Culture issue, 121–23
writing for *Xtra*, 172–74
writing *We See Each Other*, 12–13, 15–19
Annan, Nicco, 199
Anything's Possible (film), 136
Anzoategui, Ser, 198
appropriate attire policy,

24. *See also* Morehouse College
Aquaman and the Lost Kingdom (film), 169
art, trans representation in
Black drag characters, 74
explicit trans identification, 70–71
in film, 64–74
making trans experiences palatable, 64–66
regarding problematic elements, 71–73
reviewing models of possibility, 64
RuPaul consideration, 74–81
seeing fullness of oneself, 81–83
seeing oneself, 59–63
transvestism as safe sex, 66–70
articles
"Bachelorette (That Used To Be A Bachelor), The," 5
"Game Changers," 114
"Transgender Tipping Point, The," 113–14
"'Double-Sexed' Defendant Makes No Hit With Jury," 33
"Ex-GI Becomes Blonde Beauty," 95
"Guy Turned Girl Seeks Love on Reality TV," 95
"Male Shake Dancer Plans to Change Sex, Wed GI in Europe," 32
"Man Who Lived 30 Years as a Woman, The," 30–31
"Man Who Thought Himself a Woman, The," 28–29
"Woman Who Lived as a Man for 15 Years, The," 33–34
As Told by Ginger, 60

aesthetics, nonbinaryness, 201–5
Ashe, Nicholas L., 186
Associated Press, 91
Atwood, Jensen, 60
authenticity. *See* Hollywood, trans storytelling in; depicting trauma, 137
awards
  BET, 166
  ecosystem of, 166–68
  Emmys, 111–12, 115, 120, 124, 133, 163, 166, 169, 172, 216
  GLAAD Media Award, 94, 110
  GLAAD Special Recognition Award, 149
  Gotham Awards, 134, 220
  Grammys, 166, 220
  Independent Spirit Awards, 134
  Legacy Awards, 219
  LGBTQ Visibility Awards and Reception, 150
  NAACP Image Awards, 166
  Oscars, 11, 16, 48, 50, 52, 70, 115, 127, 132, 134, 137, 152, 161, 163, 166, 172, 179
  #OscarsSoWhite, 59, 166
  Trailblazer Award, 219
Ayers, Robyn, 13

B
Baig, Bilal, 205
Bailey, Fenton, 75–76
Baker, Rick, 52
Baker, Sean, 134
Banks, Tyra, 87, 88, 90
Baszile, Natalie, 184
Beane, Douglas Carter, 67
Becoming Chaz (film), 99, 193
"Becoming Him," TEDx Talk, 189
Beek, James Van Der, 161
Bendix, Trish, 180

Benet, BeBe Zahara, 83
Berendt, John, 64
Bernier-Clarke, Aubree, 198
Berry, Halle, 152–53
"Beyond Representation" (essay), 137
Beyond the Gender Binary (ALOK), 199
Big Momma's House (film), 52
big-footed bitches (BFBs), 117
Billboard, 78
Billings, Alexandra, 114
Billions, 145, 197
Billy Budd (film), 70
Bingham, Margot, 161
Binnie, Imogen, 159
Birth of a Nation, The (film), 48
Black Jorgensens. *See* Jorgensen, Christine
Black List, The (documentary), 117
Black masculinity, 181–84
Black on Both Sides: A Racial History of Trans Identity (Snorton), 34
Black people 30, 53–55, 89, 107–8, 112, 143, 172–73, 182, 187, 216, 224
Black trans people 10, 33, 54, 93, 102–4, 108, 118, 135, 149, 166, 172–73, 181–82, 187–88, 192
Black trans power, 14–15
Black womanhood, 54, 172–73
Black, Georgia, 30–31
#BlackGirlMagic, 72
Blake, Marsha Stephanie, 102
Blanco, Mykki, 198
Blank, Radha, 161
Blige, Mary J., 78
Blue Bloods, 188
Bob the Drag Queen, 198
Bogle, Donald, 54

Bold and the Beautiful, The, 216
Bold Culture, 137
Bond, Julian, 143
Bono, Chaz, 99–102, 179, 184, 217–18
born in the wrong body, phrase, 89
Bornstein, Kate, 163
Boy! What a Girl! (film), 48
Boys Don't Cry (film), 11–12, 179
Brady Bunch Movie, The, 78
Brandon Teena Story, The (documentary), 192
Brevard, Aleshia, 115
British Independent Film Awards, 220
Broadnax, Willmer "Little Axe," 14
Brooklyn Liberation March, 13–14
Brooks, Danielle, 107
Brown, Ava Betty, 31, 33
Brown, Carlett Angianlee, 31–32
Brunson, Quinta, 207
Bryant, Chandler, 61
Butcher, River, 198, 203
Buzzfeed, 78
By Hook or By Crook (film), 120, 192
Bynum, Juanita, 22

C
Caldwell, Sandra, 115
Call Her Ganda (film), 155
Calvo, Javier, 215
Campbell, Naomi, 62
Campbell, Tisha, 219
Canals, Steven, 157
Cannes Film Festival, 127
capital. *See* money, trans representation influenced by
Cardasis, Damon, 164
Cashier, Albert, 29
Cayne, Candis, 69
CBS, 100, 102, 115, 125, 152, 159, 216

Chappel, Tim, 70
Chappelle, Dave, 52, 138
Chasez, JC, 91
Chester, Rodney, 60
Chicago Daily Defender, 33
Children of a Lesser God, 190
Chilling Adventures of Sabrina, 198
cis, 29, 53–54, 89, 95, 103–4, 111, 120, 124–32, 147–48, 154, 158–59, 163, 165, 167, 200
City on a Hill Press, 61
Civil War, 29
Clarice, 152
Clifton, Lucille, 140
Clinton, Bill, 95
Coel, Michaela, 207
Colby, Kerri, 80
Coleman, Drew, 61
Combs, Sean "Diddy," 110
Complex Canada, 206
coronavirus, 171
Cossey, Caroline "Tula," 114
Cousin Skeeter, 60
Cox, Laverne, 9, 94, 98, 121–23, 172, 182
  "Ain't I a Woman? My Journey to Womanhood," 107–9
  debuting on *I Want to Work for Diddy*, 110–11
  hosting *TRANSform Me*, 111
  importance of role of, 115–16
  interviewing, 116–21
  on *Law and Order: Special Victims Unit*, 111
  on *The T Word*, 111–12
  Time article, 112–16
Crayton, Jazzmun Nichcala, 73, 115
Crooklyn (film), 78
cross-dressing
  Black man playing Black woman character, 50–54
  as career path, 44
  as comedic factor in film, 45–50

outlawing, 28–29
perceived emasculation, 53–56
performances before film, 43–44
race films and, 48–49
in Shakespeare works, 44
tracing contemporary beliefs, 45–46
Tyler Perry as Madea, 39–43
vaudeville, 44–45
weakening Hays Code, 49
Cruz, Eliel, 13
Cruz, Wilson, 60
CSI: NY, 74
Curtis, Tony, 49
Cusack, John, 65

D

Dallas Buyers Club (film), 131, 163
Dancing with the Stars, 99
Danish Girl, The (film), 131
Darling, Candy, 115
David Makes Man (film), 179
Davis, Alex Blue, 179
Dawson, Ellis C., 61
Deadline, 129
Defining Moments with OZY, 175
De Los Santos, Brian, 149
Deveau, Chablis. *See Midnight in the Garden of Good and Evil* (film)
Devereaux, Shaadi, 137
Devin-Norelle, 198, 204
Disney
  nonbinaryness in, 203
  villains, 204
Dhont, Lukas, 127
Diary of a Mad Black Woman (play/film), 40–43
Different World, A, 82
Dillon, Asia Kate, 145, 179, 197, 220
DiMarco, Nyle, 189
Directors Guild of America, 117

Dirty Sexy Money, 69
Disclosure (documentary), 48, 57, 99, 146–47, 149, 151–53, 155
divas, 128
Dix, Peyton, 13
Don't Ask, Don't Tell, 95
Dorsey, Omar, 186
Doubt, 159
drag queen, term, 64, 66
Drag Race Thailand, 79
Dressed to Kill (film), 50
Du Bois, W. E. B., 143
Duplass, Jay, 120
Duplass, Mark and Jay, 134–35
DuVernay, Ava, 102, 114, 185–86

E

Eastwood, Clint, 64
Ebony, 30, 33–34, 114
Ek, Daniel, 138–39
Elbe, Lili, 31
Elise, Kimberly, 43
Ellis, Aunjanue, 102
Emerald Point N.A.S., 115
Emmys, 115
Empire, 61
Employment Non-Discrimination Act, 182
Encyclopedia of Vaudeville, The (Slide), 45
Entertainment Weekly (EW), 75, 129, 197
Equal (documentary), 36
Essence, 114, 172–74
Euphoria, 216
Ewell, Dwight, 73
Exonerated Five, 160

F

Faking It, 190
Fayaz, Mohammed, 13
Feder, Sam, 48, 151
Fernandes, Marriska, 206
Filippo, Fab, 205
film
  cross-dressing in. *See* cross-dressing

indie films, 16, 161, 181, 220

trans storytelling, 127–40

Five Wells, 143. *See also* Morehouse College

Fleming, George S., 46

Fletcher, Elliot, 190

Floyd, George, 13

For the Boys, 61

Ford, Tyler, 99

Ford, Yance, 48

Forney, Ali, 88

40-Year-Old Virgin, The (film), 74

Forty-Year-Old Version, The, 161

Fosters, The, 191

Foxx, Jamie, 52, 54

Framing Agnes (documentary), 36

Franklin, Aretha, 128

Franklin, Robert Michael, Jr., 154

Free CeCe! (documentary), 118–21, 124

Fresh Air, 75, 76

Future of Trans, The, 153–54

Fysh N Chicks, 92

G

Gardiner, Lizzy, 70

Gardner, Dawn-Lyen, 186

Gay & Lesbian Alliance Against Defamation. *See* GLAAD

Gay Agenda, The (film), 67

gender nonconforming, 15, 18, 37, 116, 131, 133, 144–45, 154, 159, 163, 173, 205–6

Gender Outlaw: On Men, Women, and the Rest of Us (Bornstein), 163

Gender Reveal (podcast), 198

gender, assigning. *See* cross-dressing; tracing contemporary beliefs

gender, performing, 23. *See*

also Anderson, Tre'vell: in church

Getting Curious With Jonathan Van Ness, 37

Getty Images, 117

Girl (film), 127–32, 139

Girls, 188

GLAAD, 10, 93, 98, 99, 100, 110, 115, 163, 188, 191

"Where We Are on TV," 136

Studio Responsibility Index, 136

Glee Project, The, 99

Glen or Glenda (film), 10, 49–50, 57

God's Tabernacle of Prayer Church of Christian Fellowship, 21–25, 41–43

Golden Globes, 69, 120, 163, 171–72

Gonzo (Muppet), 203

Good Girls, 179

Gotham Awards, 134, 220

Grammys, 220

Grant, Cary, 49

Green, Misha, 207

Green, Rashaad Ernesto, 134

Greenfield-Sanders, Timothy, 116–17, 145, 159

Grey's Anatomy, 179

Griffith, D. W., 48

Gross, Terry, 75

Guardian, 80

Gun Hill Road, 134

H

Hall, Irma P., 72

Hall, Thomas(ine), 26–27

Hamburger, Christian, 32

Harsh Reality: The Story of Miriam Rivera (podcast), 96, 105

Hart, Alan L., 31

Her Story (web series), 141, 216

Heredia, Wilson Jermaine, 73

Hernandez, Greg, 95

Hiding My Candy: The

Autobiography of the Grand Empress of Savannah (Chablis), 66

Hillz, Monica Beverly, 80

HIM *(The Powerpuff Girls)*, 201–2

history, trans visibility, 21–25

Black gender transgressors, 29–34

Civil War, 29

dispelling rumors, 25–26

earliest recorded transgressor, 26–27

outlawing cross-dressing, 28–29

women enlisting as men, 27–28

Hitchcock, Alfred, 50

Hoffmann, Gaby, 120

Hollywood Foreign Press Association, 171

Hollywood Reporter, 100, 101, 132, 133

Hollywood, trans storytelling in. *See* film

depicting trauma, 132–37

lack of trans movie star, 136–37

money as influence, 137–40

reviewing *Girl*, 127–32

Holmes, Dorothy M., 21–22, 41–43

homosexuality, 45

House of LaBeija, 164

House of Xtravaganza, 164

How to Be You: Stop Trying to Be Someone Else and Start Living Your Life (Marsh), 198

Howard, Silas, 120

Howley, Jim, 94

I

I Am Cait, 98, 120

I Am Jazz, 98

I Can Do Bad All by Myself (film), 39–40

I May Destroy You, 207

I Want to Work for Diddy, 94, 98, 114
I Was a Male War Bride (film), 49
In Full Bloom: Transcending Gender (documentary), 74
In Living Color, 52
Independent Spirit Awards, 134
Indiana University Bloomington, 114
Instagram, 152

J

Jackson, Brandon T., 52
Jackson, Dominique, 157, 159, 171
Jackson, Maynard and Samuel, 143
Jackson, Randy, 91
Jakes, T. D., 22
Jamal, Fatima, 144, 153
Janssen, Famke, 102
Jeffersons, The, 10
Jenner, Caitlyn, 9, 98, 120, 134
Jennings, Jazz, 98
Jerome, Jharrel, 102
Jerry Springer, 182, 185, 217
Jet, 32
Jeté, Kornbread "The Snack," 80
Johansson, Scarlett, 131
John Wick: Chapter 3 – Parabellum (film), 179
Johnson, Marsha P., 14, 64
Jones, Imara, 153
Jorgensen, Christine, 31, 49, 95, 113
Joseph, Channing Gerard, 29
Judith of Bethulia (film), 48
Julian, Jonathan, 60
Jung, E. Alex, 81
Juwanna Mann (film), 52

K

Kenan and Kel, 60

Keith, Gregory, 60
Kidron, Beeban, 66
Kiki (documentary), 175
Kim, Christine Sun, 190
King Ester, 9
King, Aliya S., 24
King, Isis, 10, 87–91, 182
King, Martin Luther, Jr., 143
Knickerbocker, 28
Kohn, Mitch, 67
Kumu Hina (film), 36

L

L Word: Generation Q, The, 179–81, 191
Lady Chablis, The, 65–66
Landecker, Amy, 120
Late Late Show with James Corden, The, 171
Latino List, The (documentary), 117
La Veneno. *See* Rodríguez, Cristina Ortiz
"Laverne Cox on Her Career Journey, from OITNB to Inventing Anna" (video), 125
Law and Order, 111, 188
Lawrence, Martin, 52, 54
Lawson, Bianca, 186
Lawson, Richard, 79
Lee, Mekhai, 61
Lee, Spike, 78, 143
Legendary, 91
Leguizamo, John, 66
Leibovitz, Annie, 76
Lemmon, Jack, 49
Leon, Francis, 44
Leto, Jared, 128
Lettin' It All Hang Out (RuPaul), 78
LGBTQ Visibility Awards and Reception, 150
Library of Congress, 49
Lifford, Tina, 186
Light, Judith, 120
Lil Mama, 91–93
Lindo, Delroy, 78
Little Prince, The (film), 115

Living Single, 114
Livingston, Jennie, 158
lolly, 92
Los Angeles Daily News, 95
Los Angeles Times (LAT), 9, 62, 101, 116, 128–30, 133, 144, 146, 163, 164, 172, 180, 186, 216, 217
Lovato, Demi, 198–99
Love, Kylie Sonique, 79
Lovecraft Country, 207
"Lovin' Is Really My Game," 83
Lubin, Siegmund, 46
Lynch, Lashana, 172
Lysette, Trace, 96

M

Madea (character), 39–43
Madea Cinematic Universe. *See* Perry, Tyler
Madea Goes to Jail (film), 94
Madea's Witness Protection (film), 43
Madgett, Carl, 182
Madonna, 92
magazines, 34, 169
Magnolia Pictures, 134
Major, Miss, 14
Making His Band, 93
Maldonado, Leiomy, 91–93
"Male Shake Dancer Plans to Change Sex, Wed GI in Europe," 32
Maltin, Leonard, 50
"Man Who Lived 30 Years as a Woman, The," 30–31
"Man Who Thought Himself a Woman, The," 28–29
Man-Made, column, 189
Man, Chella, 122, 189–91
Mann, Tamela, 41
Marie Claire, 159
Marsh, Jeffrey, 198, 204–5
Martin (show), 52
Martin, Eugene, 32
Marymount Manhattan College, 114
masculinity, discourse, 181–84

masculinity. *See* transmasculine people

masquerade laws, 28

Matrix Resurrections, The, 191

Matrix, The, 159

Matsoukas, Melina, 172

Maury, 182, 217

McBee, Thomas Page, 180

McCracken, Craig, 201

McCraney, Tarell Alvin, 179

McDade, Tony, 13

McDonald, CeCe, 118–21

McHarris, James (Jim), 33–34

Mean Girls (film), 24

Medicine for Melancholy, 207

Meet Me at the Fountain (short), 46, 48, 57

Men of Morehouse. *See* Morehouse College

Mendoza, Kalaya'an, 13

Midnight in the Garden of Good and Evil (film), 64–66, 85

Milan, Amanda, 121

Milan, Tiq, 179, 188

Minaj, Nicki, 75

Miranda, Lin-Manuel, 171

Mitchell, Kel, 60

Mitchell, Louis, 182

Mo'Nique's Fat Chance, 185

Mock, Janet, 113, 159–60, 172

Moesha, 60

money, trans representation influenced by, 140

Monroe, Marilyn, 49

Monsecour, Nora, 127. *See also Girl* (film)

Moonlight (film), 161–63, 179

Moore, Adrienne C., 107

Moore, Indya, 158, 163, 169–70. *See also Pose*

Morehouse College, 14–15, 23–25, 82, 112

Morgan, Tracy, 52

Morley, Angela, 115

Motion Picture Production Code (Hays Code), 49

Motocrossed (film), 203

movies. *See* film

Mrs. Doubtfire (film), 50, 67

MTV Movie & TV Awards, 220

Mukerjee-Brown, Lucy, 117

Murphy, Eddie, 52

Murphy, Ryan, 157, 158

Murray, Pauli, 14

Myra Breckinridge (film), 50

N

NAACP Image Awards, 166

Nash, Niecy, 102

National Association of Black Journalists (NABJ), 148, 150–51

National Association of Hispanic Journalists, 148

National Film Registry, 49

National Gay and Lesbian Task Force, 178

National Transgender Discrimination Survey by the National Center for Transgender Equality, 177–78

NBC, 119, 159, 179, 188

Nef, Hari, 215

Netflix, 16, 48, 52, 102, 107, 129, 131, 138–39, 152, 179

New Girls on the Block, 98

New York Daily News, 95

New York Times, 70, 133, 150, 159

NewNowNext, 116

No Fats, No Femmes (documentary), 144

No Ordinary Man, 193

No Time to Die (film), 172

Noah's Arc, 60–63, 73, 81

nonbinaryness
characters teasing, 201–5
creating *Untold Stories*, 197–200

Disclosure significance, 151–53

discovering, 143–48

importance of Monica Roberts, 148–51

in *Sort Of*, 205–7

term, 145

Uncle Clifford, 195–97

visibility of, 143–55

nonnormative, term, 25, 45

Norman, Tracey "Africa," 169

Núñez, Miguel, Jr., 52

Nutty Professor (franchise), 52

O

Obama, Michelle, 184

Old Maid Having Her Picture Taken (short), 46

oppressors, 9
in Bible, 41–42

Orange Is the New Black, 94, 107, 113, 115, 124, 158

Orange Is the New Black: My Year in a Women's Prison, 107

Out, 104, 114, 121–23, 128, 190, 219

Out in Hollywood (blog), 95

Out List, The (documentary), 117

Outfest, 116–18

Oxygen, 185

P

P-Valley, 195–97, 208

Page, Elliot, 152, 197

Pan African Film Festival, 74

Paris Is Burning (documentary), 92, 158, 175

Parkers, The, 60

passing privilege, 98

Pearce, Guy, 70

Peirce, Kimberly, 11, 179

Perry, Tyler, 39–43. *See also* Madea (character), 54

Peters, Evan, 160

Pharoah, Jay, 52

Picardi, Phillip, 121–22, 189, 197
Pier Kids (documentary), 175
PinkNews, 97
Pitchfork, 78
podcasts, 18, 37, 96, 97, 105, 166, 197–98, 202, 208
Polk, Patrik-Ian, 60
Porter, Billy, 136, 158, 166–68
Porter, Edwin S., 46
Pose, 61, 175
  after end of, 168–74
  Michaela Jaé Rodriguez, 161–65
  overlooking performances, 166–68
  reception of, 157–61
Powerpuff Girls, The, 201–2
Prancing Elites Project, The, 98, 105
problemasia. *See* art, trans representation in
Project Runway, 93
Psycho (film), 50
Punks (film), 73–74

Q
Queen & Slim (film), 169
Queen Sugar, 184–88, 193
Queen, The (film), 84

R
race films, 48–49
Rae, Issa, 114, 207
Ramos, Dino-Ray, 130
Random Acts of Flyness, 154
Rashad, Nicholas, 182
Razor Tongue, 216
reality TV, trans visibility in
  on *America's Best Dance Crew*, 91–93
  on *America's Next Top Model*, 87–91
  images of trans women, 97–99
  lack of focus on trans men, 99–102

There's Something About Miriam, 96–97
Transamerican Love Story, 94–97
Recess, 60
Redefining Realness: My Path to Womanhood, Identity, Love & So Much More (Mock), 159
Redmayne, Eddie, 128
Reign, April, 166
Reign, Eva, 136
reporting, transphobia in, 113–14
representation, 9–10, 49, 63–64, 72–74, 98, 109, 149, 158. *See also* trans visibility
retraumatizing, 103–4
Revolutionary War, 27–28, 29
Reynolds, Chloe, 61
Reynolds, Ryan, 152
Rhimes, Shonda, 114
Ri'chard, Robert, 60
Rich, B. Ruby, 215
Richards, Jen, 216
Richter, Dora, 31
Ridloff, Lauren, 190
Rios, Jorel, 91
Rivera, Miriam, 96–97
Rivera, Sylvia, 14
Roberts, Monica, 34, 109–10, 148–51
Robinson, Jackie, 31
Rocket Power, 60
Rodriguez, Chi-Chi. *See To Wong Foo, Thanks for Everything! Julie Newmar* (film)
Rodríguez, Cristina Ortiz, 215
Rodriguez, Jason A., 157
Rodriguez, Kitana Kiki, 132
Rodriguez, Michaela Jaé, 158, 161, 164–65, 166–67, 171–72. *See also Pose*
Rogan, Joe, 139
Ross, Angelica, 150, 159,

169. *See also Pose*
Ross, Tracee Ellis, 152
Royale, Latrice, 83
Rub and Tug (film), 131
RuPaul, 74–81
  catalyzing cultural conversations, 79
  problematic conversations, 79–81
  on pronouns, 78–79
RuPaul Show, The, 78
RuPaul's Drag Race, 64, 75, 79, 83
RuPaul's Drag Race: All Stars, 79
Ryan, Marja-Lewis, 180

S
S. D., Trav, 44
Sahar, Hailie, 159, 170–71. *See also Pose*
Sailor Moon, 203–4
Sampson, Deborah, 27–28
Sanchez, Deshawnda "Ta-Ta," 120–21
Santiago, Renoly, 73
Sarandos, Ted, 138, 152
Sarony, Gilbert, 46–47
Saturday Church (film), 161–63
Saturday Night Live, 52
Sawyer, Diane, 120
Schmider, Alex, 99
Schofield, Scott Turner, 179, 216–17
Scholder, Amy, 151
Schunard, Angel Dumott, 73
Scott, Amiyah, 125
Scream: The TV Series, 198
Sea Squawk, The (film), 48–49
Sea, Daniel, 180
see yourself, phrase, 59
Selma (film), 186
Sense8, 159
Sevigny, Chloë, 179
Shakespeare, William, 44
Shameless, 190
Shamir, 198, 203

She-Ra and the Princesses of Power, 198

Sheng, Leo, 180

Shirtliff, Robert. *See* Sampson, Deborah

"Short History of Trans People's Long Fight for Equality, A," 57

Showtime, 179–81

Silence of the Lambs (film), 202–3

Simmons, Kimora Lee, 62

Sir Lady Java, 14

Siriboe, Kofi, 186

Sissy: A Coming-of-Gender Story (Tobia), 130, 198

Sister, Sister, 75, 78

Slide, Anthony, 45

Small Town Security, 99

Smith, Brian Michael, 180, 184–88

Smith, Danyel, 166

Smith, DD, 93

Smith, Sam, 197

Smith, Willow, 91

Smith, Zeke, 99–102

Snipes, Wesley, 66, 68

Snorton, C. Riley, 34

So Popular!, 159

Soldier's Girl (film), 95

Soloway, Joey, 119–21, 147

Some Like It Hot (film), 49

Sort Of, 205–8

Spacey, Kevin, 65

Sparks, Shane, 91

Spearman, Doug, 60

Spectrum, 137

Spielberg, Steven, 67

SpongeBob SquarePants, 204

Spotify, 138–39

Stafford, Zach, 130

Stamp, Terence, 70

Stannard, Isaiah, 179

Star, 125

Starr, Dennis, 99

Steinmetz, Katy, 113

Stephens, Darryl, 60

Steven Universe, 198, 208

Stevenson, ND, 198

Stewart, Ianne Fields, 13

Still Black: A Portrait of Black Transmen (documentary), 181–84, 192

Strut, 105, 171, 185

Stryker, Susan, 48

Studio City, 216

Sugar, Rebecca, 198

Sullivan, Jayla, 93

summer of racial reckoning, 13

Sundance, 132–34, 151

"Supermodel (You Better Work)," 78

Surpassing Certainty: What My Twenties Taught Me (Mock), 159

Survivor: Game Changers—Mamanuca Islands, 99–102

Swank, Hilary, 11, 179

Swann, William Dorsey, 29

Swayze, Patrick, 66

Swift, Taylor, 128

Switched at Birth, 189

T

T Word, The, 111–12

Tales of the City, 179

Talley, André Leon, 61, 81, 118

Tambor, Jeffrey, 120, 128, 163

Tangerine (film), 132–37, 141

Tao, Mimi, 93

Taylor-Klaus, Bex, 198

Taylor, Breonna, 13

Taylor, Mya, 132

Teena, Brandon, 11, 179

Television Academy, 166

television, trans visibility in, 136. *See also* reality TV, trans visibility in

Thayer, Timothy. *See* Sampson, Deborah

There's Something About Miriam, 96–97

Thomas, Lia, 183

Thompson, Kenan, 52

three-article rule, 28

tick, tick . . . BOOM! (film), 171

Tijssens, Angelo, 127

Time, 9, 10

Tirado, Fran, 13

Titans, 189, 190

To Wong Foo, Thanks for Everything! Julie Newmar (film), 66–70, 78, 85

Tobia, Jacob, 130, 198, 203–4

Tootsie (film), 50

Training Day (film), 121

trans antagonisms, connecting cross-dressing to. *See* cross-dressing

Trans Awareness Week, 107

transcestors, 210–14

trans femininity, centering of, 183–84

trans history, learning, 34–35

Trans List, The (documentary), 117, 124, 145, 159

trans visibility, 7–19

in art forms, 59–85

creating timeline of, 9–11

cross-dressing, 39–56

early examples of, 21–35

in Hollywood, 127–41

Laverne Cox, 107–25

negative byproducts of, 217–18

nonbinary visibility, 143–55, 195–208

Pose significance, 157–74

post-*Time* erasure of, 112–16

in reality TV, 87–105

transmasculine people, 177–93

Transamerican Love Story, 94–97, 98, 110

Transcendent, 98

transfirmative action, policy, 120, 147

TRANSform Me, 111, 124

transgender tipping point, 9, 101–2, 119, 122, 132, 139, 181

transgender, term, 146

TransGriot, 15, 34, 109–10, 149–51
TransLash Media, 96, 153
transmasculine people
  challenging invisibility of, 189–91
  considering, 177–81
  depicting meaningfully, 184–88
  discourse on masculinity, 181–84
Transparent, 9, 119, 133, 147, 158–59, 163
TransTech Social Enterprises, 169
Trap Door: Trans Cultural Production and the Politics of Visibility, 218
travesti, term, 43–44
Trump, Donald, 102, 160
2020 Presidential Candidate Forum on LGBTQ Issues, 169

U

Una Mujer Fantástica (film), 9, 141
Uncle Clifford. *See P-Valley*
Underground Railroad, The, 207
Underwood, Blair, 102
United States
  Black gender transgressors in, 29–34
  Civil War in, 29
  earliest documented gender transgressor in, 26–27
  outlawing cross-dressing in, 28–29
  trans killings in, 183–84
  women enlisting as men in, 27–28
Untold Stories: Beyond the Binary (web series), 197, 208
Untold Stories: Beyond the Binary (podcast), 197–200
Usdin, Carly, 198

V

Valdez, Rain, 219
Vanity Fair, 76, 120, 152
Variety, 45, 159–60
vaudeville, 44–45
Vega, Daniela, 9, 141
Veneno, 215
Vibe, 24
Vida, 198
villains, Disney, 204
Vincent, Christian, 60
Visage, Michelle, 78
Vogue, 61
Vogue Evolution, 91–92
"Vogue," 92
Vulture, 81

W

Wachowski, Lana and Lilly, 159, 191
Walker, Lamont, II, 61
Walters, Barbara, 98
Watch Out for the Big Grrrls, 93
Watson, Lachlan, 198, 202–3
Wayans, Shawn and Marlon, 52
Weaving, Hugo, 70
Webster, Devon, 91
Welch, Jay, 181
Wells, Ida B., 149
Wesley, Rutina, 186
When They See Us, 102–4, 105, 172
When We Rise (miniseries), 74
"Whip My Hair," 91
White Chicks (film), 52
White Famous, 52–53
White Men Can't Jump (film), 68
white people, early US trans visibility of, 26–29, 161
Whitney, Oliver, 132
"Why it's time Hollywood let trans voices tell, and embody, their own stories," 146

Wiley, Samira, 107
Williams, Malechi, 91
Williams, Robin, 67
Williams, Serena, 184
Willis, Raquel, 13–14, 172
Wilson, Ajita, 115, 149
Wilson, Flip, 50–52
Winchell, Barry, 95
Witherspoon, Reese, 61
"Woman Who Lived as a Man for 15 Years, The," 33–34
womanhood, 23, 30–31, 54, 64, 92, 107–8, 172–73, 183–84
Women's List, The (documentary), 117
Wonder Woman, 204–5
Wood, Ed, 10, 49, 57
Woodard, Alfre, 78
Woodstock, Tuck, 198
World According to Garp, The, 10

X

Xtra, 151, 172–74
Xtra Magazine, 143
Xtravaganza, Jose, 164

Y

Yellow Submarine (film), 201
Younes, Samy Nour, 57
Young, Ethan Thomas, 181

Z

Zak, Laura, 216
Ziegler, Kortney Ryan, 179, 181
Zoolander 2 (film), 136
Zora, 92